DADDY DRINKS

Six Dads Trying to Get It Right—While Getting It Hilariously Wrong

By Henry Dittman, Padraic Duffy, Victor Isaac,
Michael Lanahan, Jacob Sidney, and French Stewart

Post Hill

PRESS

Published by Post Hill Press
Printed in the United States of America

FOREWORD

I knew, for some time, that my son and five of his friends were writing a book about raising their children. So when they asked me to write a foreword to their enterprise, I, of course said I would be honored. I have now read the entire book.

Oh my God.

They say it takes a village to raise a child. But not if it is the village *idiots*. This "How to…" travesty should only be read in your rear view mirror as you race away from every suggestion or insight they propose. I shudder to do the math of how many children these five men currently are in charge of. And they might even make more. The horror.

Now, perhaps I might bear some responsibility when it comes to Padraic's behavior and his ideas on how to raise youngsters. There was that time when walking from the car to the house with him in the pitch black night, I suddenly dropped his hand, screamed "werewolf!" and ran as fast as I could into the darkness. He just shrieked, dropped to the pavement, and laid there in a fetal position. But that was just one time. Over the years I have received several cards and ties for Father's Day. I'm pretty sure he got over it.

So now here I sit at my computer, wondering what is to be done. But then I picture, so vividly, the two kind, loving grandchildren my son and his amazing wife Emily have gifted me and my wife with. And I know the parents of his friends feel the same way about their grandkids. And it makes me think that no matter how ridiculously boneheaded a dad might be, if there is a strong thread of uncompromising love between him and his child, then the result can't be all that bad.

So knowing the love that these six fathers have for their children, I can only say, "Well done, idiots. Well done."

One proud Grandpa,
Patrick Duffy

INTRODUCTION

The six of us go back a ways.

Long before any of us had children—or even knew the amazing women who would make that happen—we were friends. Buddies who stayed out into the wee hours drinking, and making theater, and drinking while making theater. We were actors and writers in L.A., living the life.

And then suddenly, out of nowhere, there was a shit-pot of kids. With the craziness of managing our kids' schedules (not to mention our own careers), we obviously weren't able to hang out the way we used to. We were stuck bottle feeding our kids in the middle of the night, or shuttling them to music class in the afternoon, or wringing out dirty cloth diapers in the toilet first thing in the morning. And we loved it (except for that last part). But we couldn't help but realize:

The days of drinking together were gone.

Until one day when the newest dad needed some help, and we realized we didn't have to leave the house to be together. With a stocked bar and some WiFi, we could imbibe and talk about our kids all night on instant messenger. (What else is there to talk about?) And most importantly, we could have each other's backs when the going got tough.

And that is how *Daddy Drinks* was born, and this is the instant message thread, typos and all.

P.S. None of us are baby doctors. Follow our advice at your (and your child's) own risk. This is just the shit that worked for us. Enjoy!

IT ALL BEGAN WITH A QUESTION ABOUT SWADDLING

HENRY: Daddy to Daddy thread. That's what this is. Each of you said I could ask you questions concerns or just call if I needed support. Seems like you guys might need that too, and you're all great dads!

This is my question today. Hannah screams bloody murder every time I take off her swaddle. I read in happiest baby on the block babies hate being on their backs, plus she's only three days old and had a very traumatic birth, womb poop and cord around neck we had to emergency c section, i'm just curious if you have encountered this any of you? I'm sure there's nothing wrong with her, but will she ever stop screaming her head off every time I change her out of her swaddle?

The GOOD news is that 99% of the time a tight swaddle really chills her out.

The other good news is that she breast-feeds like a champ, so we have ways to soothe her. Just looking for some perspective!

6:54am

MICHAEL: I haven't had that experience, but as far as I'm aware from Happiest Baby, it's okay to keep her in the swaddle for long periods right now. Also remember the technique he showed you, where you can use a swaddle cloth to tie her on to you (skin-to-skin) which might swaddle her and provide another carrying option.

Hopefully, she's just transitioning and the screaming will cease as she eases into the world a bit more. Also try those other four "S"s from Happiest Baby to see how those help. Another option: Finley really responded well to being in the dark bathroom with the fan running. Good luck!

6:59am

HENRY: Huge help last night was Sarah sleeping in the rocker skin to skin. I've done all swaddles and diapers since she's on bed rest but this way every hungry cry and diaper doesn't destroy sleep or half-sleep I guess.

Happiest Baby works it's amazing, by the way!

7:00am

HENRY: These moments help!!!

7:45am

MICHAEL: Also, I hear Womb Poop is playing Coachella this year.

8:01am

HENRY: They're great. Cord Throat is too Agro for me.

8:18am

PADRAIC: I remember every diaper change being a scream fest. We would blast a cheap noise machine (we stole it from inside of a teddy bear) that played ocean waves right by his head. The rhythmic shushing was helpful too. Also, the sound of a hair dryer will soothe them (just make sure it's aimed away!)

8:41am

VICTOR: First off, I love the fact that this thread started at 6:12am, while I was in the shower after having "overslept." Secondly, Alex hated being naked in the beginning. He would scream bloody murder every time we changed his diaper or gave him a bath. I can't remember when it calmed down, but it did. I think it was after he pooped in the bath.

8:48am

JAKE: Henry I'm so sorry for what you and Sarah went through. That's awful. We had a planned c section, but crystal had complications after the delivery and was on the table for another 5 hours. Blue wouldn't breathe so she went in the NICU . Longest night of my life. Anyway, happiest baby on the block is the bomb. It's the only system I put any credence in, personally. So I'm sure you'll be fine. You'll also probably come to appreciate just how low previous generations set the bar. Being a great father mostly requires paying attention and responding. Its difficult but it's not actually complicated. In another month or so you can start trying to take her for walks in the stroller or strapped to you. In the meantime you will become the fastest baby burrito maker in the West. I hope in a few weeks we can come visit you and bring some soup or something.

Give sarah our love.

8:50am

VICTOR: Oh, and that's a great picture! I want to eat her cheeks!

8:52am

JAKE: 👍

3

1:58pm

MICHAEL: Yeah! Those goddamn cheeks already!

2:20pm

FRENCH: We were 6 weeks early and 10 days in the NICU. 4lbs 3 ounces. The only class we had taken was on nursing and at the end Vanessa said "Fucking Hippies. If a cat can figure it out..."

5:08pm

HENRY: And damn I just got home and read the whole thread, jake and French my heart is aching. I was in scrubs with no warning losing my mind but I immediately was holding a baby and scream across the operating room, through tears, "she's beautiful baby, she's healthy!" I can't imagine the waiting. For both your daughters and your wives. Heartache.

I'm glad I started this thread. It's true the bar is low. I feel guilty I'm not doing more with help from family, they're saying they've never seen a man do so much. Then again? During my birth or my sisters My mom sent my dad home to watch the series finale of gunsmoke because there were no vcrs and he couldn't be in the delivery room anyway. The first time i soothed my baby girl (happiest baby is the shit) and she snuggled into my neck? I was fucking done. Drinks soon yes oh yes.

5:08pm

HENRY: Anyone got a great sleep system? Book to read or video to watch for when we start that in three four months???

5:12pm

MICHAEL: Sure do. But we'll cross that bridge.... you've got some time.

6:52pm

JAKE: We've been very fortunate with sleep... There have been rough patches, but she mostly trained herself...

7:31pm

VICTOR: Ditto what Lanahan said, you gots plenty o'time don't even sweat it. Now is the time to put that surfing experience to good use. You caught the wave, now just ride it in, because really the first three months is just survival. You have no control.

2:20am

FRENCH: Tight swaddle. Skin to skin. Patience when it all goes to fuck town and no one is having an experience like yours.

BUTTONS ARE BABY HITLER

1:31am

FRENCH: Oh! Henry. This is possibly the most important thing to know. When choosing a bedtime pajama? Go with zippers! You don't want to navigate 9000 tiny snaps at 4 in the morning. Zipper onsey!

1:35am

PADRAIC: Yes on zippers. Even worse than snaps? Fucking buttons.

1:38am

FRENCH: a button is baby Hitler.

6:32am

HENRY: Already on my shit list? Any item for a newborn that is a pullover. Who's the the dick face who thought my baby would like THAT? Zippers yes.

7:41am

MICHAEL: Buttons and snaps make me want to punch a baby. Not really though. Unless they deserve it. They know what they did. Am I right?

BABY POUNDAGE IS A TERRIBLE PHRASE

2:24pm
PADRAIC: Let's add up our babies' birth weights and see how much baby poundage we have made!

2:24pm
VICTOR: lol

2:24pm
PADRAIC: Baby poundage is a terrible phrase.

2:25pm
FRENCH: Net weight at birth? Or current, sweet ass, baby poundage?

2:26pm
PADRAIC: If it's current weight, we can keep a ticker going!

2:27pm
FRENCH: Okay. Report your baby poundage

2:28pm

VICTOR: Wait, current weight or birth weight? I got lost
Birth weight was 7 pounds even

2:29pm

PADRAIC: At birth: 6.2. Current:32 pounds!

3:27pm

MICHAEL: 7lbs 10 oz. for Cheeks McGee Lanahan. current 19lbs 9 oz.

4:42pm

HENRY: 8 lbs 2.9oz. That's right. Decimals are funny and I just added one to the total.

6:52pm

JAKE: 6lb 8oz then... 19lb 1oz now...

10:40pm

FRENCH: So Freddy- 32 pounds Hannah May - 8 pounds 2 ounces Blue- 19 pounds 1 ounce Helene Claire - 15 pounds. Cheekc McGee 19lbs 9 oz. Victor- report your current baby poundage!

9:42am

VICTOR: Is it bad that I have no idea how much Alex weighs? We obsessed about it for months, then went a little too obsessive, so we stopped thinking about it. I think he's around 21 pounds or something.

10:44pm

HENRY: French? Hannah is 8 lbs. 2.9. oz. I really think you either round up or use the .9

You know what? If you guys aren't going to take these stats seriously? Them I'm just... You know what?

(Slams door)

By the way? My girl handled a changing today with NO screaming freakout. She also garnered points for sleeping on my chest.

10:49pm

FRENCH: Hannah has just been downgraded to 3 grams. (Slam)

10:50pm

HENRY: Dammit, Hannah, you brought this shame on our family. You know what? I'm just... You know what?!

10:53pm

FRENCH: And now she weighs the same as cotton.

10:53pm

HENRY: YOU do.

Sorry about the whole "you weigh as much as cotton," French. That's not what I wanted this thread to be about. Not one bit.

10:54pm

FRENCH: And now you're both morbidly obese.

10:54pm

HENRY: Mother FUCKER. Nah, you're right.

10:59pm

FRENCH: A baby snoozing on your chest. Nothing better.

THE FIRST
FEW DAYS

11:22am

VICTOR: By the way, Ditty, how you guys doing on food? People bringing you enough? Do you need anything?

4:13pm

HENRY: We have a food tree going and if you want to come say hey and bring food we'd love it!!!!

8:21pm

MICHAEL: Parenthood means...sometimes not being able to brush your teeth until you've been up for a couple hours...*sigh*

8:35pm

HENRY: Our first week home? I didn't brush my teeth until bedtime every day. It was fucking weird.

9:20pm

VICTOR: I think we were 4 days in before my first shower.

9:31pm

PADRAIC: We're supposed to brush our teeth?

THE CHOCOLATE LOTTO

10:32am

JAKE: Here's something no one tells you: how much time you will spend at a literal standstill, watching poop come out of her butt, waiting to make sure she's done... (answer = a LOT)...

10:33am

HENRY: HA!!!! Before we figured out burping, all her poops we're blowouts. Merconium EVERYWHERE, so I got to anticipating. This was a fools errand.

10:36am

VICTOR: You're not done with blowouts my friends! Though I will tell you we found blowouts were more common when Alex was reaching the top end of his diaper size. So we started switching to the bigger size at the bottom weight recommendation.

His shit literally had no where to go but up!

10:51am

PADRAIC: I am in love with you guys.

11:04am

FRENCH: Vanessa and I play a game called The Chocolate Lotto. It's basically trying to sand bag the other person into changing a dirty diaper. Vanessa saying "Aw. I think she misses her father." I fall for it and I'm on mud patrol.

11:11am

MICHAEL: My wife literally cannot handle Downtown Brown (as we call it). Our deal: I'll handle poop, but she's going to have to handle vomit. I think I win?

11:12am

PADRAIC: It's not about winning; it's about making the other lose.

We use reusable diapers. I spray shit into the toilet and wring the diaper WITH MY BARE HANDS!

11:13am

MICHAEL: The poop right now is Good Poop. Once she starts on formula or real food. It becomes Bad Poop. Deeply Bad Poop. I long for breastmilk poop.

Yeah, I said it.

11:56am

VICTOR: Cindy is really good at making me deal with the poop. She just sort of disappears and then I smell it.

Not sure if she's dropping a bomb before leaving the room just to force the issue or if she's good about being down wind of Alex so she smells it first.

12:58pm

MICHAEL: Daddy Tip #32: OxyClean is amazing at getting out poop stains, fecal stains, shit stains, & that wine you spilled on your daughter's onesie that one time.

1:09pm

HENRY: That ONE time, Lanahan?

1:57pm

FRENCH: Helene once shat out the back of her "I love my mommy" pajamas. And rather that deal with it? I ditched em in the trash. Her "mommy love" will have to be assumed.

2:12pm

VICTOR: Ditching pooped in clothes is the right thing to do sometimes. I used to keep scissors in his diaper bag, so if it was too much to deal with I'd just cut off the onesie.

11

2:13pm

FRENCH: Like a MASH unit surgeon.

2:14pm

PADRAIC: You'll definitely need scissors to cut them out of poop filled pull-ups. (The straitjacket of diapers!)

2:15pm

JAKE: At 4 months I heard a shocked "Oh my God!" from Crystal in the next room. I entered to find her in mid-change, Blue giggling hysterically, Crystal with a horrified look on her face... and followed Crystal's gaze down along a 6-foot stream of liquid poop Blue had apparently just launched across the fancy down comforter of the Palm Springs vacation home my mom had rented... Happy Birthday Nana!

2:17pm

FRENCH: HAAA!!! Nana- "Why am I not getting my deposit back?"

2:19pm

JAKE: Poop stream, mom... adorable granddaughter poop stream...

2:38pm

HENRY: Nana needs to watch her mouth and be glad she's involved at all!

Scissors in the diaper bag is genius.

So you guys are telling me that my baby that is sleeping 18 hours a day right now is about to become a demon?

When the hell does that happen?

2:58pm

MICHAEL: They use their sleep to plot their poopy schemes.

4:24pm

JAKE: 👍

5:26pm

HENRY: You guys are legends. This is great for me, truly.

BABIES IN THE SINK

HENRY: Baby bathed in the sink. Straight up country.

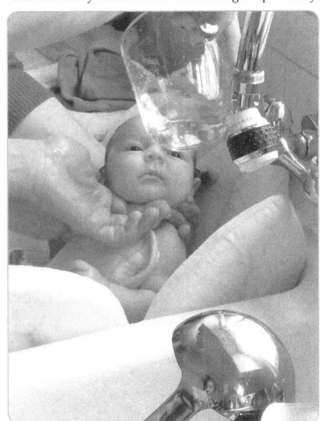

8:41pm

JAKE: Are you rinsing Hannah with a rocks glass? Straight-up gangster, Ditty…

10:34am

FRENCH: After a long shooting day, bathtub time might not be so glamorous.

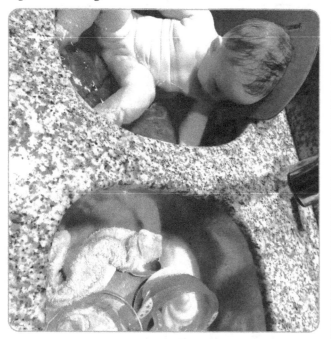

11:38am

JAKE: 👍

11:39am

JAKE: The spray nozzle comes in very handy…

1:30pm

FRENCH: Correct, Sir.

2:07pm

HENRY: Holy. Crap. She needs to do those dishes while you bathe her. Contribute to the household, little baby!

4:17pm

PADRAIC: I'm hoping the disposal is on the dish side. Please tell me the disposal is on the dish side.

4:44pm

HENRY: Raise your own kid, Duffy.

Seriously though. The disposal IS on the dish side right, French????

4:49pm

JAKE: Then where would the poop go?

4:57pm

PADRAIC: Guys- I'm pretty sure we're the best dads ever.

POOP IN THE PANTS

6:13pm
HENRY: Drumming out a rhythm while you rock back and forth to the beat, in the corner, in fetal position, endlessly?

6:31pm
HENRY: Singing Christmas carols nonstop from December first til February 1st and maybe March 1st at this rate?

6:35pm
HENRY: Trying to use the force to levitate a holiday popcorn tin?

7:17pm
VICTOR: nope nope and nope.

8:35pm
FRENCH: Cookie?

8:42pm
VICTOR: What?

10:53am
HENRY: Dude? You gonna reveal the alex photo answer or what???

11:07am
VICTOR: Pooping. The answer was pooping.

11:53am
MICHAEL: Well, he's got the squat down, so that's progress towards incorporating the toilet, I guess.

9:08pm
JAKE: On Friday at the Smart & Final in Fresno, my daughter pointed and said, "Pooping."
She was right. her butt... she pointed at her butt…

9:31pm
PADRAIC: Ten minutes ago, my son took a dump in his toy story undies. To add flair, he was wearing a plush bathrobe and a crown.

9:34pm
HENRY: Hard to top that.

9:36pm

PADRAIC: And he has started trying to "wipe" himself without telling us after secret poops. I put "wipe" in quotes because it is just indiscriminate smearing. It's like a tramp stamp of poop.

Stink ink.

10:15pm

MICHAEL: I'm so happy I don't have the poop stories to compete with your caka-children. (yet)

BABY LAW

MICHAEL: I'm on a bit of an emotional roller coaster this morning. Tomorrow my baby will be one year old. Exactly a year ago, my wife became the most powerful person I know as she screamed this blob out of her. This curmudgeonly, wrinkly baby. I've experienced more in this year than I have the last five. (and this last one year has felt like five.) One day I'm so in love I think my heart can't contain it, the next I'm considering going out for milk and not coming back. Actually, it's not really day-to-day, so much as moment-to-moment.

It's been one long year, and I still can't believe she's mine, that I made this, that I have to guide this person.

Am I babysitting someone else's kid?? For God's sake, when are they going to pick her up already? I need a vacation! I've learned new definitions for the words: Patience Unrelenting Fatigue Pride I'm not sure it's gotten easier, but old things are easier and new things are more difficult. Having gotten through it, I think I look at the future with a bit of relief. That little girl is all mine Thanks, Daddies, for the last few months - you can't imagine how helpful it's been.

Baby Law

10:34am

MICHAEL: (Thanks for letting me blurp all over this thing)

10:34am

FRENCH: Baby Law, Mike.

10:35am

HENRY: Straight Baby Law. Defined.

11:50am

VICTOR: #daddydrinks

INAPPROPRIATE BABY USAGE: HEISMANING!

3:02pm

HENRY: Crack kills

3:34pm

MICHAEL: COIN SLOT!

4:43pm

HENRY: Take it easy, mike!

7:18pm

HENRY: Actively side holding and shushing in photo!

7:21pm

PADRAIC: 👍

8:02pm

MICHAEL: Excellent Heisman-ing of the Baby!

8:10pm

JAKE:

8:12pm

VICTOR:

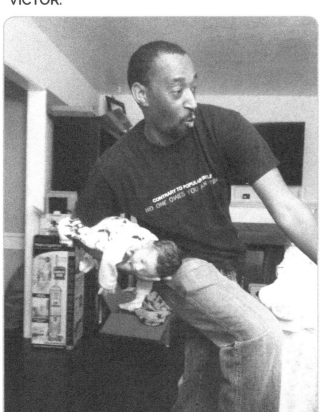

8:42pm

MICHAEL:

9:04pm

PADRAIC:

9:15pm

FRENCH: Welcome. Welcome to inappropriate baby usage.

Really proud.

A CONFUSION OF NIPPLES

7:57am

HENRY: Dear drinking daddies.

Is there any reason to not use a pacifier? We are finding that when she's rooting but doesn't want the boob it calms her, but I'm worried she'll get addicted to it. Thoughts?

8:07am

JAKE: We went all in on the paci, for her comfort and our sanity... Blue is a regular Maggie Simpson... If you can minimize it, more power to you…

8:37am

MICHAEL: WE tried to fight against it as much as possible, because of the crutch-factor. That being said, we occasionaly gave it to her. Luckily, or perhaps because of this, she's never been a big user. More often than not we would give her our pinky and she would just suck away. I actually miss that so much... A good rule of thumb is to give her the pacifier and if she falls asleep you can take it out, or if it falls out just leave it.

9:33am

VICTOR: Sucking is a very comforting thing for babies, so it's no surprise it calms her down. We were also worried about the pacifier addiction, but we decided that we would do what it took to survive the first 3 months and then adjust after that. After three months, I was back at work and unfortunately working 60 hours a week, and Cindy couldn't stand to give him anything except her boob. So, he no longer accepted the pacifier and unfortunately, the bottle as well and has never looked back.

9:45am

MICHAEL: I 2nd that first three months is survival. Just get through it - I remember reading that it's too early to form bad habits.

9:51am

HENRY: Thanks guys!

10:01am

VICTOR: Yes, I remember that too. It's not until about 6 months...or maybe 9 that they start forming habits.

10:04am

VICTOR: Also, some people worry about nipple confusion with the pacifier, where the baby won't take the breast anymore. But they don't get anything out of the pacifier, so there's not really a danger of them preferring that.

10:06am

PADRAIC: The pacifier was the most important object in our house...for just a few months. Then he got tired of it. But I can't imagine getting through those few months without it. I feel like that has happened with a lot of things. Your whole world is about a white noise machine, or a pacifier, or one specific toy. And then just like that, you can't remember when you stopped using it.

10:07am

PADRAIC: I, however, got nipple confusion.

I went to town on a box of number 2 pencils thinking they were attached to my wife.

10:15am

VICTOR: Ha!

I had nipple amnesia. I forgot what one looked like without a baby attached to it.

I kept pinching my wife's nose. She was not amused.

10:18am

PADRAIC: Nipple Confusion will be the name of our jam band.

10:20am

VICTOR: Yes!

11:48am

HENRY: Bless you mike.

1:05pm

JAKE: Our breast feeding experience was super traumatic for both of them, so I think we gave in a little more than we might have otherwise on the paci just so we wouldn't feel like we were torturing her any more... Now it's a falling asleep thing...

1:06pm

HENRY: Yeah I'm not looking forward to that battle. Lanahan lent me Sleep Easy solution just so I can start getting some Information and look for patterns and ideas.

Gratefully, UCLA and our pediatrician both have lactation consultants on staff which has helped a lot.

2:24pm

PADRAIC: Nipple Confusion: (Noun) 1. When a baby finds it difficult to latch on to breastfeed because of prior bottle use. 2. The reason you give your wife when she catches you with a stripper's boob in your mouth.

10:58am

MICHAEL: I can't wait to go near my wife's nipples again. I think I can see them on the horizon.

THE NON-BABY ARM

9:10pm

FRENCH: That's the stuff.

9:11pm

HENRY: I was side hold soothing and thought "why the fuck can't I work in the yard too?" What you can't see is I also had a pacifier in with the thumb of my holdin' arm.

9:11pm

VICTOR: All you need is a beer.

9:12pm

HENRY: Had a whiskey waiting on the kitchen counter. My non baby Arm was holding the hose.
Wow talk about a setup.

9:22pm

FRENCH: You will be astounded at what you can do with your non baby arm. I regularly leverage a milk bottle from the side of my face to her mouth and drink a beer at the same time.

9:42pm

JAKE: Experience with one-handed web surfing comes in really handy with a newborn.

10:21pm

FRENCH: That's the truth, Sidney.

Inappropriate Baby Usage II: Mustard that Baby!

10:13pm
MICHAEL: Mustard that damn baby.

11:40pm
FRENCH: Yes. Mustard her, Henry.

12:30am
JAKE: Mustard. Go.

2:33am
HENRY: I don't know what that is. Just tell me what to do!

6:56am
HENRY: For the love of God what is mustarding? Because I changed two diapers PACKED with it yesterday.

MICHAEL:

8:26am

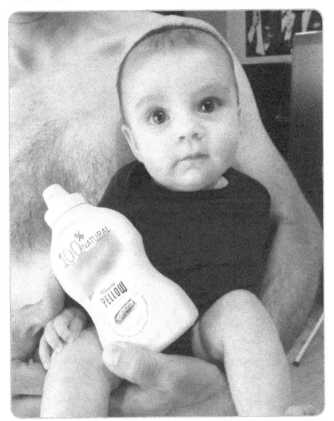

VICTOR:

8:49am

9:24am

HENRY: holy crap. how did this start??? or do i have to post to get the origin?

10:05am

MICHAEL: I couldn't even tell you how this shit started...My brain is mush.

10:57am

HENRY: Au natural.

10:58am

VICTOR: LOL!

I can't remember if it was French or Jacob who first mustarded their baby, but it was the next in line after we heismaned out babies. Followed by the much less successful famous moments in sports, with your baby.

11:21am

HENRY: Yeah I don't watch college ball so that was my heisman. Whaddayagonnado?

Jake. French. Repost em. I'm delighted by this crap. Especially that they're clueless about it all. Alex looks thrilled. Finley looks like Finley.

3:02pm

JAKE:

3:03pm

JAKE: It was me. I was first. I may not have a lot to claim in this crowd, but I'll be damned if anyone takes mustard baby away from me.

3:04pm

JAKE: It was in response to something Lanahan wrote on someone else's thread about Jack Daniels' mustard...

It had nothing to do with the baby initially, she just wouldn't let me put her down at that moment...

the rest = history...

3:06pm

VICTOR: Is that how it started?!?!?! Hahahaha! Then we all went shirtless.

3:37pm

HENRY: Jake? You have a LOT to claim with this group. Plus you're a charter member!!!

5:55pm

FRENCH: Blam!

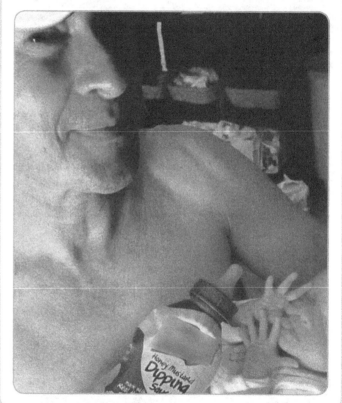

FRENCH: Mine has a nipple on mustard.

5:56pm

HENRY: Incredible.

7:16pm

[Jake named the conversation: Daddy Drinks]

HENRY: Well done jake

9:23pm

PADRAIC: I just now read the mustard stuff. I'm tempted to go wake Freddy up right now and hand him some goddamn mustard.

12:21am

HENRY: It's your privilege. And his birthright.

6:02am

PADRAIC:

6:45pm

6:46pm
FRENCH: I love the thumbs up.

7:20pm
JAKE: Padraic you're supposed to appear shirtless in the picture…

7:21pm
HENRY: Get 'im jake.

7:26pm
FRENCH: Yeah, Padraic. Some mustard, a child and a shirtless father. It's not Algebra.

7:38pm
JAKE: Padraic is also terrible at Algebra.

8:08pm
PADRAIC: Damn, you step away for a second and out come the fucking daggers.

8:09pm
PADRAIC: Double shirtless!

8:13pm

HENRY: Freddie made padraic hold the mustard.

"Dad. I'll do the photo but you gotta hold the fucking condiments."

In my mind all children are foul mouthed.

Double shirtless is epic. Touché.

8:18pm

PADRAIC: When Freddy says jump, I say good word! And then I say how high.

5:37am

HENRY: I've known you all for years. Collectively and individually? This is some of our best work.

DIAPERS OF THE CLOTH

12:17pm

HENRY: I know I'm setting myself up for ridicule here, but do any of you guys do cloth diapers? If so I have a question.

12:45pm

VICTOR: Not for Alex…

1:00pm

FRENCH: Not us.

2:20pm

MICHAEL: No thanks.

2:35pm

PADRAIC: We have done cloth diapers for the past three years and love it. We still have disposable that we used at night and for when we would be out of the house for long periods of time (or on vacation), but when we are home, it's easy. And I give a lot of credit to the cloth diapers and cloth wipes (with just water) for why Freddy has never had a bad diaper rash. We just spray them out, wring 'em, throw them in a diaper bag, and wash them in the washer. Easy peasy.

2:36pm

FRENCH: Landfills don't pollute themselves, Henry. We all have to do our part.

3:10pm

PADRAIC: I am a man of the cloth.
The priest of poop.
the Deacon of Stinkin'!

3:15pm

FRENCH: The Khaleesi of Fecies.

3:20pm

VICTOR: The Master of Meconium.
The Czar of the Brown Star.

3:21pm

PADRAIC: The Chief of Queef.

3:22pm

VICTOR: The Don of Diarrhea

3:22pm

PADRAIC: The Boss of Ass (must be said in British accent)

3:22pm

FRENCH: Did Emily's info mention that your baby will get pin poked more than a Bourbon Street Voodoo Doll?

3:23pm

PADRAIC: I am so proud of us right now.

3:25pm

FRENCH: The Shart Sheriff.

3:29pm

HENRY: Cloth diapers no longer use pins. But I will for sharts and giggles.
Also when we say diaper I'd prefer we pronounce the "i" in the middle. "Dye-a-puhr"

3:32pm

FRENCH: Baby Law

4:11pm

FRENCH: Cloth diapers have to be stapled to the baby. Fact.

4:15pm

HENRY: They GET to be stapled.

4:28pm

VICTOR: The Champion of the Corn Hole

4:34pm

FRENCH: The Ruler of Stool.

5:22pm

FRENCH: Genghis Dingus.

6:01pm

JAKE: Khal of Mal. But really Khaleesi of Feces wins this round.

We're cloth all the way. We did our own laundry for the first several months. Then my mom very generously got us a year of service. Lulu Dew. I cannot recommend them highly enough if you're going that route. Now we're back to laundering, and it's really not that bad.

6:06pm

FRENCH: I use a Huggy that turns blue when it's wet. Then I remove it, go outside and throw it in an old woman's face.

6:23pm

JAKE: I echo everything Duffy said, especially about rashes... We've had one in 18 months, and never use cream or anything (except that once) besides powder... We also use disposables out of the house, with sitters, etc... but not at night...

7:10pm

HENRY: Awesome fellas thanks. My mom is here French so she's getting a poopie diahper in her craw in five seconds.

7:19pm

FRENCH: I will drive in the rain to throw a diaper in Mother Dittman's sweet yap.

7:26pm

HENRY: Thank you for that respectful gesture upon my mom's craw. Thank you. French. Is that so difficult, guys???

11:01pm

FRENCH: I am going to have sex with all of your mothers. Trust me. I love you. This is totally cool with all of us. ♥ ♥ ♥

7:47am

MICHAEL: We use disposable, but Finley's only had one or two rashes. And those were probably because I only change her twice a day. I mean, what: am I made of diapers over here? Suck it up, baby - it's all downhill from where you are.

IS IT SIX WEEKS YET?

VICTOR: If you really want to improve your marriage, try and get it on with your wife at 3am after she just got back in bed after putting the baby back to sleep. They love it!

10:29am

HENRY: Yes. Wow. The newborn version of this is to constantly ask your wife has it been six weeks yet?

10:30am

VICTOR: Also, they can never say you don't find them attractive anymore. I never understood why she got upset when I pointed out that blow jobs were acceptable according to the doctor

10:30am

FRENCH: That's just medicine. Medicine.

10:32am

MICHAEL: Hey, remember when we used to get blow-jobs? That was great.

12:35pm

HENRY: A blow-what now? Rings a bell but not sure.

12:39pm

PADRAIC: You think you have it tough? Try convincing a vegan to swallow!

12:52pm

JAKE: Rim-shot!

1:03pm

PADRAIC: She won't let me do that either!

1:12pm

FRENCH: Vanessa is trying to lose baby weight. But I'm feeling "Not so fast." I honestly wish she would stop exercising.

10:39am

MICHAEL: Let her keep exercising, just start sprinkling weight-gain powder into her Chardonnay.

11:03am

PADRAIC: Is that a euphemism for sex?

11:04am

FRENCH: It's shocking how little we speak of our actual children. It's nipple confusion and attempts to pork your wife before she gets her junk settled. Terrible.

12:51pm

PADRAIC: Well, it doesn't matter now. My wife has absolutely no reason to ever have sex with me again for the rest of our lives.

1:28pm

JAKE: 👍

1:50pm

HENRY: 👍

2:00pm

VICTOR: It sounds like we need to make another trip to Spearmint Rhino!!!

2:00pm

JAKE: Can you talk to Crystal about what part of the budget to take that out of?

2:07pm

2:11pm

VICTOR: Daddy's don't ask for money to see stripper titties, they take it! #babylaw

2:12pm

FRENCH: Baby law! You could also argue nipple confusion.

2:21pm

JAKE: Oh wait, I know: emergency supplies…

2:45pm

FRENCH: Spearmint Rhino Manager- "Don't latch the girls!"

4:52pm

PADRAIC: I've decided that once a day I will declare to my wife that something is "Baby Law!"

1:43pm

HENRY: six weeks clearance today and I acted like I wasn't really excited. Wasn't easy. "Oh baby whenever it's right for you!"

7:24pm

VICTOR: You are a better man than I, Hank. I was all "Hey, guess what tomorrow is!?!? The day your va-jayjay is ok!!"

7:25pm

FRENCH: I just shat wine in my pants! And yes. I'm drinking wine

7:30pm

MICHAEL: (again)

8:11pm

HENRY: I have so much to learn from all of you.

8:16pm

MICHAEL: It's a bit fuzzy, but even though we tried at 6-weeks, I think we could only play "Just The Tip" for a couple weeks…

8:16pm

HENRY: C Section finally pays off babay!!!!

8:20pm

JAKE: I'd be thrilled with a bit fuzzy... I haven't seen a fresh wax in three years...

8:24pm

FRENCH: A visit from Lord Tippington is usually followed by a pronouncement from Lady Ouchington. Lady Von Shavington has left for the States.

9:59pm

MICHAEL: What a coincidence! Lady Ouchington visits the South Bay about once a week. If you ask me, she's overstayed her welcome.

10:01pm

FRENCH: 👍

RACE WAR

JAKE: Apparently Stewart's been gabbing to his wimminfolk about Daddy Drinks... loose lips, buddy... #babylaw

FRENCH: Babylaw has taken a "snitches get stitches" turn. I didn't see that coming. And now I have to join the Aryan Nation for protection. If I switch to Victor's black gang do I get a physical upgrade or just rougher treatment by the police?

VICTOR: French, by merely contemplating the change, you have made it and are now black. Good luck not getting pulled over in the nice new car. And have fun "fitting the description" of quite a few criminals!

HENRY: Oooooh I want that!

VICTOR: Ditty, you're in! Now we outnumber the whiteys! Suck it, cracka!

11:13am

FRENCH: It's been a mixed bag so far. People are locking their car doors right in front of me. But my jump shot is really landing.

11:30am

JAKE: race traitors…

12:03pm

MICHAEL: Jake's gotten really aggressive, you guys. I might have to stay in his corner. In the Big House, crazy survives.

1:33pm

HENRY: White devils.

1:40pm

FRENCH: Why is there a race war on the baby thread?

1:47pm

JAKE: "And now I have to join the Aryan Nation for protection." - French Stewart

1:48pm

FRENCH: Nope.

1:50pm

JAKE: 👍

1:52pm

FRENCH: We might all have to agree we've been "hacked" and move on.

1:55pm

HENRY: Darn hackers. Probably all white devils.

Inappropriate Baby Usage III: Fun in the Kitchen

7:32pm

FRENCH: A new meme! (babies doing dishes)

7:45pm

FRENCH: Or maybe you'd like a Babies Eating Unlabeled Roommate Food Meme.

7:46pm

FRENCH: Either way - you jackholes need to contribute some photo's .

8:57am

VICTOR:

49

8:58am

VICTOR:

8:58am

VICTOR: I couldn't remember if it was dishwasher or refrigerator, so I did both.

10:48am

MICHAEL: It was both. And you have done well.

1:07pm

VICTOR: Bonus: Alex wanted to learn how to do dishes the old fashioned way.

1:34pm

HENRY: Send him to uncle hanks house. We don't have a dishwasher yet. Other than uncle hank. So we have one. But it's often drunk on beer, scotch or power.

1:48pm

JAKE: No dishwasher and laundering your own diapers? How's your chicken coop coming along?

2:31pm

HENRY: No chicken coop but I do have a garden built and planted!!

2:37pm

JAKE: 👍

2:37pm

HENRY: ps needs some eggs? Or chickens?

Funny thing. Choice was buy the house without adding some "necessities", or don't buy a house. we'll get to those things eventually.

8:53am

JAKE:

9:49am

HENRY: Quit showing off your fancy dishwashers!!!! Please don't quit.

MICHAEL: 10:41am

10:41am
MICHAEL: "Daddy, why don't the Dittman's have a dishwasher?"

11:12am
HENRY: Fuck.

12:22pm
VICTOR: 👍

12:24pm
FRENCH: 👍

12:36pm

HENRY: Also technically this is baby with the dishwasher.

Me. I'm the dishwasher.

12:40pm

MICHAEL: "No, sweetheart, we don't need to give the Dittmans food. They're not poor, they just choose to wash dishes by hand."

12:41pm

MICHAEL:

12:43pm

FRENCH: "No, Helene. The Dittmans are Quakers and CHOOSE an appliance-less life."

1:29pm

HENRY: Dammit!!!!!!! These uppity babies think they're so much better than me.

ALONE WITH THE KID

7:47am

MICHAEL: On a serious note, gentlemen: I've just dropped my wife off at the airport for 5 days/4 nights out of town for work. So if you see that my posts are becoming increasingly manic, desperate, or gibberish, please know my daughter has won and I've lost my fucking mind.

8:57am

PADRAIC: Oh my. You will be in our prayers.

9:49am

HENRY: Dear god michael if I didn't have a newborn I'd come pitch in!!!

11:28am

FRENCH: By day 5 you'll be wearing a hat you made with foil.

11:42am

HENRY: Do NOT decide to start expressing yourself with poop diahper art, michael.

11:51am

JAKE: Caesar speed, comrade.

10:23pm

MICHAEL: Single-Daddy Journal, Entry #1: Really nailed it today. Despite the rain, we made it out for some Daddy-Daughter playground time, plus skyping with the Grandparents. Maybe this won't be so bad after all. Even treated myself to a steak and a few glasses of wine. Let's face it, I've earned it. Relationship status: It's Hero Worship. I'm a great father! (more later)

1:14pm

JAKE: 👍

1:15pm

JAKE: Oooh! I can't wait til you're eating yourself...

6:21am

HENRY: 👍

10:25am

MICHAEL: Single-Daddy Journal, Entry #2: Maybe shouldn't have had so much to drink last night. This morning her cries feel a bit more piercing...but I'm sure she's still loving our time together! Can babies judge you? Nah. It's probably just the teething. (more later)

Relationship Status: We're having fun? I'm a pretty good father.

12:08pm

FRENCH: I'm not.

10:39pm

MICHAEL: Single-Daddy Journal, Entry #3: Today we hit a couple party events. Oddly, she really seemed to cling to others, almost...desperately. We all had a great laugh at that! When we got home, she kept crawling for the door - whatta scamp! It's a grand adventure, but my head really hurts and...I'm just so tired. Looking forward to the overnight.

Relationship Status: Pretty sure I'm a decent Dad.

10:54pm

FRENCH: You killed it at two functions.

1:42am

FRENCH: You're a good dad, Mike.

6:17am

HENRY: Great dad, mike!!!!!
What's it like to go to functions?

10:42am

MICHAEL: Single-Daddy Journal, Entry #4: Last night I had a dream Finley was standing at my bedside staring at me, almost...looking down on me? When I woke I was drenched in sweat, with a pacifier in my mouth. HA! Silly dreams. I guess it must have been in the bed already. I mean, that's weird, right? Only a few more days. Pretty sure I could still nail this. Is it cold in here?

Relationship Status: Trying to maintain Daddy confidence.

10:19pm

MICHAEL: Single-Daddy Journal, Entry #5: Cabin-fever may be beginning to set in today. A UPS man knocked on our door and I started to weep. I tried to invite him in and make him a cocktail, Finley clung to him. It may have been too aggressive. In the dark I hear things. It may be a baby, or a dying seagull.

Relationship Status: Who am I? Where am I?

12:00am

HENRY: I want to want to come help you, Michael. But I'm frightened of what you'd do to me and mine. And yours. And anyone else. I speak for the group when I say please don't kill us first when you snap. Just... Don't.

10:02am

MICHAEL: SDJ #6: Fell asleep this morning during the 4:30am feed. Woke up in the crib wearing a tiny diaper (dy-ah-pur). Found Finley sleeping in my bed. I think she is in charge.

Relationship Status: I might be the baby now.

VICTOR: Goodness gracious I'm so behind on posts.

10:21am

10:47pm

MICHAEL: SDJ #7: I think my baby is talking to me. I'm not sure how - it's possibly a telepathic link - she's staring into my soul, and I'm hearing a small childlike voice. She's telling me to kill me wife when she gets home from New York. It's...it's the right thing to do. Must sleep. Just...so tired. God, my head hurts.

Relationship Status: If I do this, I could be a great dad again. I can be great again.

11:07pm

PADRAIC: Here's my kid as Sally Jessie Rafael.

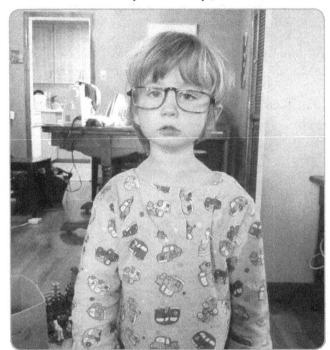

1:01am

HENRY: Padraic posting that pic was really the only logical response to mike's post.

12:43pm
MICHAEL: SDJ Final Entry: All Baby and no Wife make Mike go crazy. All Baby and no Wife make Mike go crazy. All Baby and no Wife make Mike go crazy. All Baby and no Wife make Mike go crazy. All Baby and no Wife make Mike go crazy.

5:16pm
FRENCH: Where did you bury your loved ones?

5:17pm
MICHAEL: The ocean is a very big place, French. Very big indeed.
Later…

7:27pm
MICHAEL: My wife is home, and playing with our baby. I'm making a double Old Fashioned, and I'll be damned if I don't deserve it.

7:33pm
VICTOR: #standingslowclap
LAN
A
Han!

7:51pm
FRENCH: I'm also giving Mike the clap.
Very.
Slow.

7:53pm
HENRY: You did it mike! You got the clap!

8:53pm
MICHAEL: What I've learned this week should come as no surprise to you gentlemen, but was reinforced to me tenfold. I may be tired, distracted, upset, or just rather be doing something else, but as a father you have to do what has to be done- like you've never had to before. Even at the drop of a hat. Even when it seems too hard. Even when you have to do it alone. THAT is fucking
Baby Law.

9:12pm
FRENCH: Baby Law, Mike.

9:16pm
VICTOR: Baby Law

BABY HIGH FIVE

FRENCH: 21-0 on Baby High Five.

HENRY: What's baby high five??

FRENCH: When you stroll your baby past another person with a stroller - you make friendly eye contact, hold up your hand and say "Baby High Five."

I'm 21-0. But certain people you pass by. Because they won't get it.

I'm the Phil Jackson of Baby High Five.

PADRAIC: Every time I see a dad with a stroller, I smile and say "dude- our penises work."

FRENCH: Baby High 5

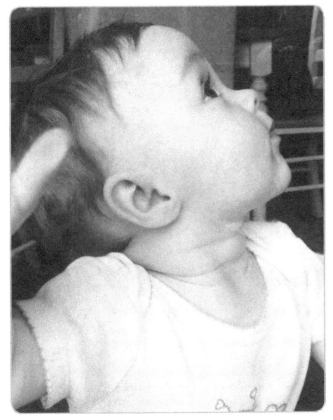

VICTOR:

6:05am

PADRAIC:

7:40am

HENRY: Hi fives ain't easy with an 8 week old but it DOES look like she's about to fist bump her kitty kat, Ray.

7:53am

JAKE: Anyone else get a distinct Shaolin vibe from Freddy's High Five?

HENRY: Yeah he has deep Kung Fu.

7:53am

MICHAEL: High Five City!

7:12pm

JAKE: Blue fully commits.

7:56am

MICHAEL:

7:12pm

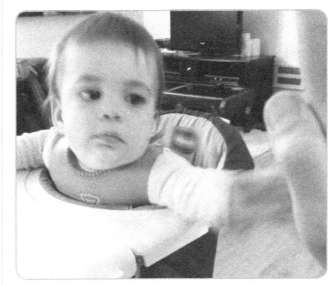

HENRY: I did it French!!!!! I did it!!! Baby high five on magnolia blvd and it felt so GOOD!!!!!

2:09pm

2:10pm

FRENCH: It's the best. You just have to size up the right people.

2:12pm

HENRY: the guy and his wife giggled. He didn't know what I was doing so I said "give it up bro."

He gave it up. Bro.

2:19pm

VICTOR: 👍

2:30pm

JAKE: 🐾

SCREEN TIME

> 7:31pm
> **FRENCH**: My baby was playing with the remote and taped Piers Morgan and the insider.

> 7:34pm
> **VICTOR**: Your baby is a commie socialist!

> 7:37pm
> **HENRY**: Next she'll want to share everyone's toys.

> 10:39am
> **PADRAIC**: I just did my first purely defensive "park the kid in front of youtube before I lose my mind" move. I can only pretend to shoot ice out of my hands for so long before I want to run down the street screaming.
>
> (Freddy has discovered Frozen, and he is OBSESSED.)

> 10:40am
> **HENRY**: Milestone.

> 10:41am
> **PADRAIC**: i mean, I have let him watch TV because I was tired, but this was a panicked move to stop going insane. But for the rest of the day, I have to address him as "Princess Elsa."

11:42am

JAKE: My mom sends me shit about limiting TV exposure. Apparently before you have a kid you're supposed to make sure you can afford full-time, high-quality child care. If I couldn't put cartoons on, I would literally never get anything done.

11:47am

MICHAEL: *sigh* so this is why I can't get any shit done. We had a pretty hard and fast NO TV rule for the first year. Our resolve is starting to break - luckily she just looks at it for a minute and then walks away. And when I say our resolve is breaking, I mean we're turning the TV on for ourselves because we're occasionally going insane.

12:39pm

HENRY: It's so funny when we were pregnant I TiVoed all these shows, thinking that I would have so much TV time because I would be stuck at home taking care of the baby. I wasn't thinking about the fact that you're not supposed to have the TV on, and truly any time it gets turned on or the phones are on she immediately stares at them and we turn them right off. Not sure how long this can last, but it is nice to watch less TV I suppose?

2:13pm

MICHAEL: Nope.
We weren't turning it on because we thought it would hurt her baby eyes and honk up her brain development. Then we talked to the doctor and she was like, "No, it can just affect their attention span a bit, and maybe their sleep if they watch a lot." "...oh."

3:10pm

HENRY: Makes sense!

3:16pm

FRENCH: I let the baby watch Caligula.

3:18pm

PADRAIC: I watched a lot of TV at first because he was so little, that he didn't even know it was on (or I could aim him away.) Then he started to actually watch, and we limited it a ton for the first year. (I would occasionally have the news on, but he didn't really care about it- it was too boring.) Now, it's just all about moderation for us. Saturday morning he gets to watch cartoons. he occasionally watches a program or two while I am making dinner. (but not regularly). He probably plays on the iPad or looks at youtube for 30 minutes a day.

3:19pm

PADRAIC: And we will watch things together a lot. So I am not getting anything done, but at least I don't have to be the source of constant amusement.

4:11pm

HENRY: Padraic that is basically how I was raised. I could watch an hour of TV in the afternoon on weekdays, I could watch cartoons before breakfast on Saturday, we watched TV after dinner as a family. I watch a lot of TV as an adult, it's been nice to not be quite so tethered to it, and I definitely don't mind my daughter starting off with a little less screen time.

4:23pm

FRENCH: We start our day with a half hour of The Hushybye's. And they are as stupid as fuck. Mop puppets that act like a bunch of assholes. They buy me time to poop and make coffee.

9:18am

MICHAEL: Finley is being a dick this morning, so once Angela leaves, The Price is Right is coming on the TV. #greatparenting

10:03am

HENRY: She needs to learn about competitive prices and gambling, mike.

7:45pm

FRENCH: Cookie Monster is as funny as shit. Just sayin'…

9:25pm

JAKE: Did you see the Cookie Monster Les Miserables spoof the other day? Epic…

9:30pm

FRENCH: Was it 24 sad Cookie Monster ballads?

7:06am

FRENCH: On the Baby Channel there is a character named Mitten The Kitten. It's a girl in a blue cat suit. And I've decided to fuck her and wreck my marriage. Bye guys.

7:20am

HENRY: Well, you had a good run. One of us has to marry Vanessa and raise your child. That's Baby Law.

7:50am

FRENCH: Baby Law. Wait. What again?
Ideally, I'd like to boink the cat and keep my wife.

8:17am

FRENCH: And boink the cat.

8:34am

HENRY: OH! Yes, sorry now I get it. Baby Law.

8:34am

JAKE: I wouldn't actually have to get divorced, so I'll take this one guys... #babylaw

8:40am

FRENCH: I find the worst shit is happening in the morning. I just gave Sidney my wife for a cartoon cat.

8:44am

PADRAIC: Check out Sheriff Callie on Disney JR. Voice of Mandi Moore. Body of a cat. Morals of a border town prostitute.

8:47am

FRENCH: That's a serious upgrade from Mitten The Kitten. Thanks for the solid.
This thread is horrid.

8:59am

HENRY: You love it more than most things.

9:02am

FRENCH: Moist things. Autocorrect.
Fuck all of you.

9:08am

JAKE: I'm just a backup plan, buddy... If you can keep your 2-D pussy quiet, I'm not gonna rat... #dontaskdonttell...

9:11am

FRENCH: Thank you. You're a majestic gentleman. And scholar of sorts.

9:25am

HENRY: This is nice.

7:49pm

PADRAIC: Right now I'm watching Doc McStuffins. That's a real show.

I watch A LOT of Disney Jr.

8:05pm

HENRY: Someday I, too, will watch weird kids shows.

8:12pm

PADRAIC: I've watched so much, sometimes I'll watch when I'm all alone.

Little Einsteins is actually a pretty good show. Sofia the First is pretty great musical theater.

I've lost my mind.

PIRATE POOP

11:40pm

PADRAIC: Today I'm downstairs while Freddy is supposed to be napping upstairs. Out of the blue , I hear him calling down to me cheerfully, "Daddy, I have poopy in my pull-ups!" I walk upstairs to find him standing on the bed, his pants and pull-ups around his ankles, a huge load of poop nestled in them like a robins egg, and he is holding to his face a pirate map. Not reading it, mind you, but pressing it to his face. So I ask you, what would have been your response?

11:42pm

FRENCH: Arrrrrrrrrrr!!!!

11:52pm

PADRAIC: Time to swab the poop deck!

1:20am

HENRY: Dear God, man, the treasure is right under your nose!!!!

9:23am

JAKE: Way to drop anchor, matey!

9:50am

VICTOR: Son, you just shit yourself. I'm not mad, but let's not pussyfoot around this situation. You shit yourself. Too direct?

10:11am

HENRY: Nope.

DISTRACTING YOUR KID

8:06pm
FRENCH: I've recently discovered I can buy myself a half hour by letting my baby tear apart a magazine.

8:19pm
HENRY: Genius.
What magazine?

8:21pm
FRENCH: People. She destroys people.

9:12pm
JAKE: There are differences between magazines?

9:13pm
FRENCH: No. He just asked so…

9:13pm
JAKE: … and French: You can totally get rid of V's extraneous paper flotsam that way… "Oh, that US Weekly? I think the baby had it… "

9:14pm
FRENCH:

9:14pm
HENRY: Also, ESPN the magazine fucking blows.

9:15pm
FRENCH: Exactly right. I fell for that. I bought it from a teen that claimed to be in a contest.

9:17pm
JAKE: #ifihadanickel

9:22pm
PADRAIC: My kid carried around a paper dinner napkin that had two stickers on it and called it his map. So...
He likes paper too.

9:25pm
FRENCH: ♥ 👍 ☀ 🍺 🍔 🍸 🐋 🍎 ☘
I just gave you all the shit.

9:26pm
JAKE: those are the most touching emoticons I've ever experienced...

9:26pm
FRENCH: I meant them.
Baby law.

9:26pm
JAKE: In the future, when someone emoticons me, I will think to myself: "Cool, but not Stewart-level"
Thank you, sir.
Baby Law.

9:27pm
FRENCH: 🌷 ☕ 🐓

9:27pm
JAKE: oh, stop…

9:28pm
FRENCH: 🐷

9:28pm
PADRAIC: I prefer to write out my emoticons.
Rose. Coffee. Chicken.

9:30pm

FRENCH: ⚡

9:31pm

JAKE: French Stewart= the Zeus of emoticons

9:32pm

HENRY: 🐘 〰

9:32pm

PADRAIC: Elephant passes wind is my Native American name.

Inappropriate Baby Usage IV: Watching Dad Poop

9:56pm

MICHAEL: I'm wondering at what point I should stop getting naked and showering in front of the baby, which I do on a daily basis. When do scarring memories kick in?

11:37pm

PADRAIC: My kid sees me naked and pooping every day. But then, so do my neighbors. And my internet subscribers.

11:44pm

JAKE: The scarring memories are kicking in right about now over here…

1:16am

FRENCH: I'm trying to figure out at what point we start judging each other. And who pulls the trigger first.

1:35am

HENRY: I can't believe you guys (looks up number to child protective services while shaking head).

1:37am

FRENCH: I just called SAG and have officially changed my name to Foster Care.

1:38am

HENRY: I expect that behavior from a Care. Especially a West Coast Care.

1:40am

FRENCH: Said the guy who attended the Harvard of Mississippi.

1:40am

HENRY: Harvard of the South, siiiiiiir! I say SIR!!!

6:35pm

FRENCH: This is what pooping looks like when mother is at Girls night.

6:43pm

HENRY: Incredible.

7:53pm

PADRAIC: Your framing is impeccable.

7:53pm

JAKE: Is that a new challenge, French?

7:53pm

HENRY: They have no idea, these ladies. Baby Challenge!!!

8:03pm

FRENCH: I'm the Ansel Adams of baby, pet, pooping photography.

8:21pm

FRENCH: But yes. Baby challenge.

6:33am

HENRY: Important to note that she was also crudding in this exact moment. Tandem y'all.

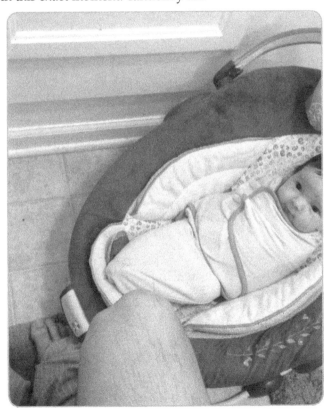

7:32am

HENRY: Dittman double deuce.

7:37am

FRENCH: That is disgraceful, Sir. Good job.

7:54am

MICHAEL: Y'know, when I gifted you that chair AND that swaddle that snuggled my sweet girl so tenderly, I never intended this, Henry. I never intended this.

8:38am

HENRY: Didn't you mike? Didn't you?
Oh you didn't? Sorry.

11:50am
MICHAEL: Finley, it's rude to stare.

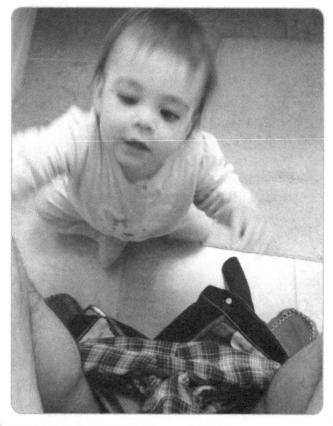

12:10pm
JAKE:

12:21pm
HENRY: 👍

4:03pm
FRENCH: The worst.

4:27pm
HENRY: Really awful.

9:14pm
VICTOR: We just had an earthquake!

12:23am
PADRAIC: God's mad at our awful conversation.

12:24am
JAKE: 😬

12:29am
FRENCH: 💩🍔 And yes I just made a poo burger.

HENRY: I blame lanahan's toilet photo.

4:10am

FRENCH: I'm in Hawaii with my wife! And we rode a zip line!

5:10am

MICHAEL: I blame French for taking his wife to Hawaii and not his Daddies.

8:14am

HENRY: And now I do as well

9:21am

VICTOR: Yeah, that was pretty selfish of French to take his wife and not us. Jerk.

9:28am

JAKE: Jerk.

9:46am

PADRAIC: He could of taken us AND his wife. No need to leave her out.

9:56am

HENRY: Unless he disagrees In 10 minutes he takes us to Bali this fall.

10:19am

JAKE: #babylaw

10:19am

MICHAEL: WE'RE GOING TO BALI! (baby law)

10:39am

JAKE: Bali Law.

10:43am

MICHAEL: (gesundheit)

10:44am

FRENCH: I'm taking you to Shut Up Town.

12:37pm

HENRY: Shutuptown, Bali!!??

12:38pm

FRENCH: Shut Up Town, Burbank.

12:39pm

12:05pm

PADRAIC: I haven't been doing these photo memes, because Freddy is old enough to ask me, "Why are you making me do this silly thing?" and I don't have an answer.

12:08pm

VICTOR: Babylaw. That's your answer. Babylaw.

12:17pm

FRENCH: "Because I said so." Baby law.

12:21pm

HENRY: Another reason to enjoy this magical time of making my daughter a part of a joke she doesn't understand.

Sniff sniff. Baby Law. Sniff.

12:55pm

JAKE: Who here has fed their baby a bottle while sitting on the toilet?

I'll start: Me. I have.

3:03pm

HENRY: Nope.

Who here is impressed and horrified? I'll start: me. I am.

3:49pm

JAKE: I like to think that's my "niche" in DD…

4:47pm

MICHAEL: My photo was my virgin baby-toilet experience. I'm very proud?

4:59pm

VICTOR: I'm ashamed to say, it was my first too…

5:36pm

HENRY: Also my first but I'm new soooo…..

6:43pm

JAKE:

2:45pm

VICTOR: You sure this is gonna make French feel better?

9:52pm

FRENCH: The baby has watched me crap like 12 times. Those days are almost over. Almost.

2:48pm
JAKE: Talk about a zip line…

2:58pm
HENRY: Hey-ohhhhhhh!

3:09pm
FRENCH: I did not see that coming today

SOLID FOOD

9:00am

PADRAIC: When they get older they become frighteningly independent. Freddy decided he would get out his own breakfast today- hummus, tortilla chips, and granulated Parmesan cheese.

9:15am

HENRY: This actually sounds like a great snack. But snacks aren't breakfast.

*Afterschool special edition of Baby Law

10:19am

VICTOR: 👍

10:27am

MICHAEL: I didn't realize we were out of oatmeal. Today, Finley's breakfast consisted of 80% puffs. Father of the Year.

10:32am

HENRY: Puffs cereal? Or puffs tissues?

10:35am

MICHAEL: I wanna say the right thing here, so…cereal?

10:51am
HENRY: Sigh. Baby Law?

11:01am
HENRY: We have oatmeal over here. Wanna come over, have breakfast, and watch Hannah for four hours while I pound beers in the garage? Baby Law????

11:52am
PADRAIC: My kid is absolutely obsessed with salmon. I broiled salmon last night with crushed garlic and soy sauce on it, and he declared that it was the best thing he has ever tasted ever. He cheered after every bite. He has recently gotten to the age where he realizes that our food is made of animals, and I have been mentally preparing how to explain it to him. (some kids do not react well.) He couldn't be happier about it. I tried to get all native american on him ("We honor the fish by eating the whole thing") and he just looked at me like I was crazy. "Mommy doesn't eat animals- BUT WE EAT ANIMALS!" (he says with a grin.)

11:59am
HENRY: Sarah is vegan. The household is mostly. Daddy is not. I look forward to the moment I have to stake my claim and I wonder how well it will go!

1:01pm
JAKE: I ate the heart of my pet sheep when I was 6. His name was Sweet Pea.

1:02pm
MICHAEL: *slowlybackingoutoftheroom*

1:05pm
FRENCH: Was this sanctioned? Did this happen at 4-H Club?

1:18pm
HENRY: Yeah jake we need more on this one.

1:25pm
FRENCH: Yeah. Was this a farming thing or should we check the crawl space for bones?

1:39pm
PADRAIC: That's Freddy's band name: Crawl Space For Bones.

1:40pm
FRENCH: Crap

1:43pm

PADRAIC: Btw, mike- that green icing from Finley's party came out of Freddy's butt looking MORE like icing. Vibrant green, soft and pliant- I was surprised it didn't have a lit candle in it.

1:48pm

FRENCH: Yeah Mike. It was Helene's first taste of icing. And it blew through her like Sherman through Georgia. A very green Sherman.

2:05pm

JAKE: Happened in my Dad's kitchen, shortly after the divorce... which seems super creepy now, but I don't think was intentional.

2:06pm

VICTOR: ...why did you eat the heart of your pet sheep? Were you trying to absorb his soft nature to tame the demon inside you?

2:07pm

JAKE: DIY hippy farm.
It was what was for dinner.

2:08pm

FRENCH: ♥ 🍔

2:34pm

HENRY: I can't believe I missed a chance to bond with you all over tinted baby diarrhea.

2:39pm

FRENCH: Not tinted. Neon. Like a shart glow stick

2:43pm

PADRAIC: His sphincter went to a rave .

2:57pm

HENRY: Dang.

2:58pm

VICTOR: I guess I missed the green party coming outta Alex's butt. I'm not sorry.

3:37pm

JAKE: No sugar = no icing = normal butt coloring.

4:04pm

MICHAEL: Wait, you guys let your kids eat that cake?! That's nuts. I wouldn't let Finley near it.

Fun Fact: that poop can be frozen and used as fondit for your next celebration cake!

YOUR PERCENTILES CAN BLOW ME

12:37am

FRENCH: Unfortunate segue.

Helene is part of a Cedar Sinai preemie study. They called because its roughly 6 months from the time she should have been born.

Dr Green- Does she roll from stomach to back?

French- (Super long pause) She's cruising. And by cruising I mean she climbed up my track suit like a monkey and "pants'd me."

Dr Green. (long pause) I'm sorry. I have to skip 25 questions.

Then the next day the pediatrician told us she was at the 50% with "normal" babies.

And I thought- "Fuck that. My preemie has the Kung Fu. Give it a minute. You'll see. Your normal % can blow me."

1:02am

FRENCH: There's a part of the "measurements" that makes me feel like they're obliged to put Helene at a numerical disadvantage and it both crushes me and makes me feel defensive and aggressive. Ta da!

1:25am

JAKE: I had a goofy busy day, but I've been reading along, and my appreciation for all of you continues to grow... You've reminded me to cherish what's working in my family, and not carry the hard parts too heavily... 'cause this shit is fuckin-A hard, no matter how you slice it... Baby Law.

1:48am

FRENCH: Baby Law.

I want to be smart. With logic and science - and if the numbers say my daughter is great? Agreed. Any thing else is not true. I'll take those facts up to the point where you don't know who we are or what we do as family everyday.

1:53am

FRENCH: I'm probably being an asshole. But I don't like people sizing up my baby. Especially when she's killing it. It just sets me off.

2:15am

JAKE: She's blowing up the experts' predictions... She's the Dayton of preems... With that, I proceed into what I'm certain will be 5 consecutive hours of glorious sleep... well done Stewarts...

2:17am

FRENCH: Love brother. She's Wichita. The Shockers?

Close as I could get

5:45am

HENRY: All those percentiles are garbage. These babies we got are all miracles. Like its a miracle you didn't beat that idiot about the neck and shoulders with his clipboard. Or hers. Or its. Baby Law: percentages only count when they're awesome. And our babies are 100% awesome.

✌ ✹ ✹

(Shocker?)

10:12am

MICHAEL: It makes me think of an old doctor appointment when the doctor said that by our next meeting (two weeks away), she should be able to pull herself up, and if not maybe we should consider seeing a specialist. Needless to say, Finley was not close to pulling herself up. Despite our best intentions, we couldn't help but let that shit get into our heads. And worry. And stress. And will we need a specialist?? Lo and behold two days before appointment, she crushes it by pulling herself up to get at a little boy. Good thing?

10:29am

PADRAIC: Don't be hesitant to say "No." We say it to our pediatrician all the time. Freddy was late to speak. Our doctor wanted to put him in a headstart program because he wasn't using enough words. We told him no to his face- we know our kid, and we know he is perfectly fine, but just taking a bit longer than your chart says he should take. I never used to think parental intuition was legitimate (and I obviously don't agree with parents who refuse serious medical advice, like inoculations) but in a lot of ways, I know more about my kid than any doctor. And now, Freddy has turned into Walt Whitman, stroking his beard and commenting on the shape of the moon. So suck it, Doctor!

11:13am

MICHAEL: I think I see Freddy's next Halloween costume!

11:22am

HENRY: His beard is so thick and bushy. It immasculates us all.

10:46pm

MICHAEL: Thanks for today, guys.

1:21am

HENRY: Sorry to have missed Finley's party, mike! Still too soon for big events with us but sending you Angela and Finley love love love.

8:36am

HENRY: i look at you guys hitting the one year mark and it seems impossible. we're at 7 weeks today and it seems like no time sort of, but MOSTLY it feels like an eternity. i started this thread because i respect and love you cats, i'm so glad it's become so much more. baby law.

7:35pm

FRENCH: Baby Law. You'll be loose soon, Henry. But it was good to see all the dudes. Thanks Mike.

12:11pm

PADRAIC: Henry- wait until they hit 158 weeks. Btw, Freddy likes to call nipples "apples." And he won't stop talking about my "pee hole."

89

12:25pm

FRENCH: Morning nap.

12:41pm

HENRY: Now those are some nice apples French!

90

CHEST SLEEPING

1:43am

HENRY: Tonight my baby would only sleep if I held her. So she slept first shift on my chest. I dozed in and out til it was Sarah's turn and now I wish I'd kept her. She hasn't slept on my chest since she was two weeks I bet. Sweetest damn thing in my life to date.

1:47am

FRENCH: It's the finest thing, Henry. It's the biggest satisfaction I've ever felt.

4:24am

FRENCH: There is nothing better than a weird little head nuzzling in on you. Inches from sleep.

My love for small theater has been replaced by baby law. Baby law is high art.

1:35am

PADRAIC: Sleeping on the chest is heaven. But Just wait until they say out of the blue "I love you daddy." In one moment, All the sleepless nights are worth it. And then they vomit 4 pounds of raspberries on you.

1:38am

FRENCH: I literally splorped beer on my lap.

1:48am

HENRY: When she's like that but turned sideways and head tucked under my chin and I'm rubbing her back, I never want the moment to end.

1:51am

FRENCH: No finer moment. It's the most personal, quiet thing in the world. I want to give her cigarettes so as to stunt time.

I think that's right.

1:52am

HENRY: Baby cigarettes? Billion dollar idea.

1:53am

FRENCH: Baby Smokes!

9:42am

JAKE: Face in the neck, conked out. There is no finer moment. It's when my life makes the most sense.

11:16pm

MICHAEL: I'm behind on photos, but I managed to capture a rare and wonderful neck nuzzle this morning. And I'll take it anytime, night or day, seven days a week:

11:19pm

FRENCH: Damn Straight. The best. Hard fought.

11:25pm

PADRAIC: Yes.

6:26am

HENRY: By the liiiiiiiight Of the silvery friiiiiiiidge.

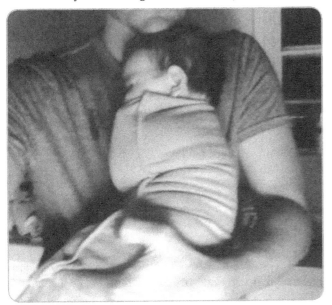

SHAKE THAT BABY!

11:16pm

FRENCH: If the baby doesn't stop crying I'm going to put her in the dumpster. Thoughts?

I'm looking for all the pamphlets the hospital gave me about not shaking the baby but.....

Seems like it's "baby shakin' time."

Right?

Okay. I'm shaking the baby and we'll play catch up ball tomorrow.

Cuz for now?

Time to shake...

That....

Baby!!!

1:09am

PADRAIC: If you turn the baby upside down, it sounds like rain.

I'm drunk.

6:53am

HENRY: We assumed.

I feel like if we ALL shook our babies it'd be okay. How do we coordinate that with lanahan on the east coast?

FRENCH: Yeah. Padraic is drunk. That's a "Lay up." As for Lanahan, I think a "baby shaking face time."

6:59am

HENRY: The wonders of the modern age!

7:15am

MICHAEL: I just shook my baby - but three hours ahead of your babies. Next time we'll skype.

I also can't wait to shake my baby at 35,000 ft. tomorrow.

8:56am

PADRAIC: It's better than shaking 35,000 babies one foot off the ground.

11:13am

HENRY: Perspective.

11:24am

FRENCH: Well, I have two choices.

2:30am

1- Treat a baby with the patience, understanding and dignity that is clearly the right of a small person figuring out the gift of life.

Or

2- Squeeze inconvenient baby with giant man hands.

HENRY: The hospital said a lot about not shaking baby. I don't remember any literature about not squeezing baby.

6:59am

JAKE: Crystal's favorite part of every doctor visit is how persistent they are in making sure no one is threatening her or the baby physically... Everyone gets that, right? It's like, boilerplate stuff... right?

3:17pm

VICTOR: ...sure....every time we go. They totally ask us that...

3:20pm

psst...don't tell Jacob, but they never ask me that and I married a white woman....

Shh! here he comes!

3:52pm
HENRY: Now I don't feel threatening and bad-boy enough!

4:56pm
MICHAEL: Also, maybe don't attend the doctor visit in a wife-beater. Drinking a beer. Threatening your wife. Holding your baby by the ankle.

5:09pm
FRENCH: No.

5:09pm
HENRY: French!!!

5:10pm
FRENCH: Nope.

5:20pm
VICTOR: Come on!!!

5:23pm
FRENCH: Good day.

5:31pm
HENRY: Huh.

5:33pm
FRENCH: I SAID GOOD DAY!
(Door slam)

5:36pm
JAKE: French seems kinda angry...

6:47pm
HENRY: Freeeeeheeeeench.

7:10pm
FRENCH: (French hides behind a plant)

7:27pm
HENRY: Huh. Look at that dry plant. Looks like it needs a'waterin'.

8:15pm
MICHAEL: Why is the plant asking for a Vodka Martini? Is this the best plant ever?

8:16pm

HENRY: Guess I'll snuggle with this lonesome houseplant. What harm could it do?

8:19pm

FRENCH: Get the balls a little. The plant balls.

8:21pm

HENRY: Well it seems like this plants needs it's balls got a little so im'a get um!

8:23pm

FRENCH: Also the plant has nipples.

8:33pm

HENRY: Sigh. Okay guess I'll just tweak these botanipples.

8:36pm

VICTOR: This plant seems to have a spigot. I'm going to try and yank it out.

8:45pm

HENRY: Have a drink it's hot out!
No love for "botanical nipples"? Botanipples???

12:43am

PADRAIC: I was gone for most of the conversation today and you all went crazy.

GOING BACK FOR SECONDS

—————— 🥃 ——————

> **7:17pm**
> **VICTOR:** DUFFY!!!!! Congratulations!!! You got the full set!

> **7:46pm**
> **HENRY:** Emily's pregnant?! Paddy!!!!!!!!!congratulations! We're so happy for you!

> **10:00am**
> **MICHAEL:** Gentlemen, I think we need to stage an intervention for Padraic. They're going back for seconds, which clearly means he's suicidal. We're here for you, buddy. We've heard your enormous cry for help. (CONGRATS YOU CRAZY BASTARD!! And you're having a girl! Welcome to the Girl-Club)

> **10:23am**
> **HENRY:** I have a sleepy newborn so I'm dumb enough to think he's making sense. Make more, paddy! Make more!!!

> **10:32am**
> **VICTOR:** 😍

VICTOR: Sleepy newborns are awesome. We aren't to the "I love you, daddy." Stage yet, but when they start running over to give you hugs....melt.
10:32am

MICHAEL: Poor Padraic. That junk was finally settled, and now...back to the grindstone. And that is a euphemism.
1:07pm

FRENCH: That's what I was thinking, Mike. Padraic was smelling hay in the stable. But then his big stupid Duffy Wang went rogue.
1:21pm

PADRAIC: Wait- it's the sex that's making these little people?!! Goddamnit. Of course! It's all starting to make sense now...
1:28pm

MICHAEL: I'll tell you what we were told while pregnant. Do as much as you can now, cuz when that (2nd!) kid comes you'll never see the light of day!
9:35am

JAKE: #oneanddone
9:39am

HENRY: #funanddone
1:09pm

VICTOR: #cumanddone
1:10pm

JAKE: #classy
1:56pm

THE QUIET HUG, PART ONE

PADRAIC: When I get a boner, Emily makes me take a time out in the corner.

JAKE: How'd you make the new one?

PADRAIC: It'll be obvious when she comes out looking like an Asian mailman.

JAKE: Or Alex Isaac.

HENRY: Yup. Classic alex isaac.

When you say "time out in the corner, we're not talking about her Lady Corner are we? Hoping the best for ya.

PADRAIC: That's kinda hot. What's wrong with me. But you can't tell me if one of your ladies sternly told you to take a time out in the corner, and she meant put your weenie in, that wouldn't be awesome.

10:07am
HENRY: It would be. The best.

10:09am
PADRAIC: But if my daughter looks like Alex Isaac, I'm coming for you, Victor. I'm giving Alex a high five, but I'm punching Victor in the face. Can you tell Saturday morning is all about cartoons? I'm just sitting here with nothing to do!

10:25am
HENRY: We're out of the house sans baby for the first time! Drunken brunch!!!!

10:46am
PADRAIC: 😵

11:09am
MICHAEL: YOU'RE DOING IT, HENRY! YOU'RE DOING IT!

11:23am
HENRY: Only talked about her for a minute. One bloody mary and one mimosa put us juuuuuust right.

11:24am
FRENCH: U
The baby typed U and sent it.
Last week she grabbed the remote and permanently recorded Inside Edition.
She's practically a Kardashian.

12:08pm
PADRAIC: Victors kid impregnated my wife, so he's one up on all your kids.

12:13pm
FRENCH: If your wife teaches a children acting camp, occasionally a very sexy toddler is going to make a move. Not his fault.

12:25pm
HENRY: It's no one's fault.

12:26pm
FRENCH: It Padraic's fault.

12:26pm
HENRY: That's fair.

6:10pm

FRENCH: Helene was about to yank the dogs tail.

Vanessa- Don't pull tail.

Me- Daddy used to pull some tail.

Vanessa- Shut your yap.

6:30pm

HENRY: Literally laughed out loud. Daddy used to pull some tail.

6:38pm

JAKE: 👍

9:05pm

JAKE: A few months ago, Blue was hammering on the wooden coffee table with some equally hard object, making an awful racket...

Crystal: Sem, will you please stop banging so loudly?

Me: It's important to learn to muffle your banging, honey.

Crystal: JA-cob!

9:08pm

FRENCH: I'm as happy as I've ever been.

9:10pm

JAKE: ☺

9:21pm

FRENCH: Vanessa has dubbed our sex as "the quiet hug."

9:21pm

JAKE: hot

9:24pm

FRENCH: It's how we got pregnant. At my moms house. The quiet hug.

9:35pm

JAKE: I'm feeling very close to the two of you now...

9:37pm

FRENCH: Yeah. I'm glad all those other assholes aren't around.

9:39pm

PADRAIC: What's up guys!?

JAKE: Well, I gotta turn in...
9:39pm

PADRAIC: 🙁
9:39pm

JAKE: Oh, no... Your poignant emoji has touched my heart...
9:42pm

PADRAIC: It's not poignant- it's my sex face.
9:43pm

JAKE: Well maybe that's something to look into, Paddy...
9:43pm

FRENCH: 👉🐷
I put my finger in a pig.
9:47pm

PADRAIC: 🐱
That's a cat dead in a pizza box
9:49pm

JAKE: 🥚
10:02pm

JAKE: That's an anthropomorphic fried egg snorting beer through his nostrils.
10:03pm

FRENCH: Goddammit.
10:11pm

VICTOR: On my way home smelling like a stripper. Saturday night successful.
2:36am

HENRY: I don't know what that means. But I love it.
6:27am

FALLING

FRENCH: Is there anything worse than watching your baby flip off a bed?

HENRY: I'm guessing no? Have you seen that? Have you all?? We have a tall bed!!! Well my wife does. I have a couch. But baby is sleeping dammit and so are we. (Dittman got a quiet hug last night btw. In his wife's bed!!!)

FRENCH: It's coming. One day she will crawl crazy faster than you clocked. And you will feel like a vagrant dad. Horrid.

HENRY: Crap.

PADRAIC: Several times when he was little, I stopped Freddy from hitting the floor by pinning him against the side of the bed. And Freddy has tumbled halfway down the stairs twice. Bloody nose, bit through his lip, had a parrot bite his finger- the kid has lived hard.

12:19am

FRENCH: You can't watch them hard enough. They fall down right in front of your face.

8:22am

VICTOR: Good lord. Now I don't feel so bad for letting Alex spin around until he was dizzy and then falling into his dresser hitting his eye on the knob. Immediate swelling and bleeding.

And I don't do so good with the bleeding. I might have freaked out a little bit.

9:00am

MICHAEL: Finley fell off the tall bed on my watch. I had never heard her scream like that ever. I was messed up aaaall day long. She may have fallen off once again - I'll never admit to that one. They suddenly get really fast...

I'm sure state school will be fine for her

9:04am

FRENCH: We dropped our babies. And now they're going to Bryman.

9:30am

VICTOR: Watching your kid eat it hard is one of the most difficult things to do.

9:35am

VICTOR: My natural inclination is to protect him from everything, but I also know he needs to figure this whole gravity and physics thing out, so I work hard at letting him do shit that makes me a bit uncomfortable. I just try and stay close and work through every possible way he can hurt himself, so I can react if necessary.

9:36am

VICTOR: But how dangerous is spinning in a circle?!? I mean at worse he's gonna throw up, right?!?

9:39am

FRENCH: Everything you said seems correct. I give you this martini 🍸

12:09pm

HENRY: As far as your baby falling off the bed and screaming loudly Mike, I think as long as they scream you know they're okay.

That might be choking I'm thinking of.

12:13pm

PADRAIC: Kids at that age are just made of cartilage. It's like tossing a shark down the stairs.

12:55pm

MICHAEL: Tossing a shark down the stairs - HA! I just splorped my non-wine.

Inappropriate Baby Usage V: Liquor Store

5:57pm

FRENCH: This is a baby in a liqueur store. You have 1 week.

5:59pm

HENRY: Holy Crap

6:04pm

JAKE: 👍

6:12pm

VICTOR: Baby in a liquor store...ok!

6:18pm

FRENCH: I really like that I don't have to defend the ethics of Baby Liquor Store Photography.

6:41pm

MICHAEL: I'm just upset we haven't come up with this sooner.

8:18pm

PADRAIC: I just need to photograph a bottle of vodka in a kids store, right? (I may be confused)

9:16pm

JAKE: Right. Go. And get documentary footage of your shoot.

9:20pm

FRENCH: I will take liqueur in a kids store or kids in a liqueur store.

9:54pm

JAKE: This thread just turned into a country song.

5:36am

HENRY: 👍

1:39pm

MICHAEL: Challenge offered, challenge met:

1:42pm

FRENCH: That just awesome parenting!!! Ha!!!

3:27pm

HENRY: Dammit we're not allowed in public yet! But yesterday our pediatrician said Sarah needs to start drinking beer at night for milk production. She asked: "Do you know what an IPA is? Henry? Are you crying? Are those tears of joy? Oh they are? You're welcome."

Or something like that.

3:54pm

MICHAEL: Guinness is real great for milk production. FACT.

3:55pm

MICHAEL: Liquor store bonus pic:"Hey, Finley, do your impression of Col. Jack E. Daniels!"

HENRY: Holy CRAP.
4:01pm

FRENCH: Jesus H Fred!!
4:03pm

HENRY: I mean, you gave the challenge and lanahan made things really real, really quick.
4:03pm

MICHAEL: Daddy-Daughter Day, baby.
4:17pm

HENRY: Meanwhile in Burbank the Dittmans are going to bed. At 8:17. Baby is sleeping we gotta cash in while the cashin's good!!!
8:18pm

FRENCH: That is correct.
8:45pm

VICTOR: Enjoy that shit while you can.
9:03pm

JAKE: 👍
9:14pm

VICTOR: I need an extension on the challenge. Alex got sick, then I got sick, so I wasn't able to get to it, but I haven't forgot.
9:36am

JAKE: New rule: no deadlines in Daddy Drinks.
10:09am

FRENCH: All I know is that Lanahan did his homework and Dittman gets a "newborn shouldn't be in a liqueur store pass." The rest of you are lazy baby meme bitches and I don't sanction your new rule. Not sanctioned.
10:17am

Except Victor. That shit is real.

Look Sidney, I don't think it's a lot to ask a sick father to take a sick baby to a downtown liqueur store. And also I would encourage all of you to get snippy with your wife at 3am because "You're sleepy and it's not your turn."

PADRAIC: Liquor is medicine! It will make you better! And always go to bed angry- that's my marital advice.
10:28am

10:28am

HENRY: That seems like solid advice.

4:16pm

FRENCH:

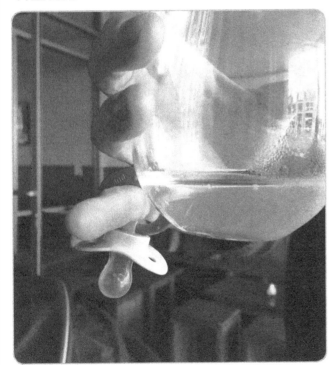

4:25pm

FRENCH:

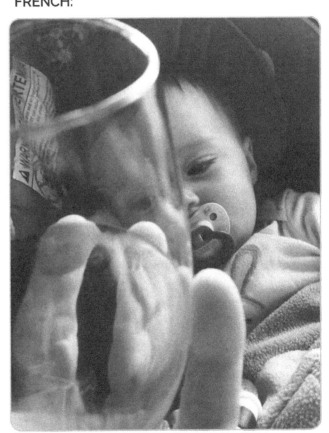

4:26pm

MICHAEL:

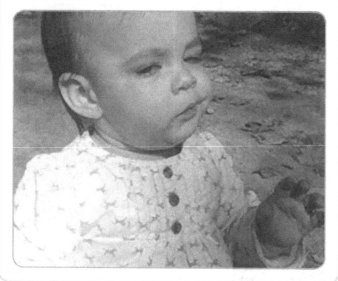

4:27pm

PADRAIC: My kid calls booze "Daddy Juice."

5:46pm

JAKE:

6:54pm

VICTOR: Our liquor cabinet is missing a handle, so it can't be baby proofed. To keep Alex out, we just put it behind the love seat in the family room. No biggie, I move it when I need to. The other day, Cindy was testing different configurations and left the liquor cabinet unguarded. Alex went straight for it, and you know what he took out? Tequila! That's my boy!

6:17pm

HENRY: Fancy!

1:38pm

VICTOR: Finally! I'm caught up on photo challenges.

9:07am

JAKE: Friday. 9am.

8:46pm

FRENCH: Awesome. Happy.

9:08am

VICTOR: 👍

10:01am
HENRY: Best.

10:07am
MICHAEL: I feel ya, Blue.

10:30am
PADRAIC: Blue label.

12:59pm
JAKE: 👍

OTHER KIDS' NAMES

—— 🥃 ——

10:59am

VICTOR: By the way, Jonas and Diane welcomed Cosimo to the world yesterday.

11:36am

JAKE: Sounds like the Olympics... "Cosimo 2014!"

11:47am

HENRY: Saw the pics that's wonderful!

11:48am

FRENCH: Cosimo Oppenheim either writes a symphony or shoots someone in the face in a Berlin hotel.

11:58am

HENRY: Yes! New chapter: other people's baby's names.

Great names: our kids' names.

11:59am

JAKE: He could do both, though, right?

12:02pm

FRENCH: Yes. "Symphony completed. Now... Unfinished business with Gustavo."

8:47pm

MICHAEL: Guys, I met a baby named Mavrick, and one named Arson. Goddammit.

8:47pm

HENRY: Arson?

Arson.

arson.

Get the Fuck outta here.

8:48pm

MICHAEL: I'l leave once assholes stop naming their kids after felonies.

8:48pm

HENRY: Not you! You can stay. Arson. They should go home and think about what they did.

10:44pm

PADRAIC: They can't go home- their kid burned it down.

6:55am

FRENCH: Grand Theft Auto Dittman.

Aggravated Assault Lanahan.

Drunk And Disorderly Sidney.

...and Got Profiled Isaac.

These are all boys names.

Except for Blowin' A Dude For Drugs Duffy.

8:34am

PADRAIC: I can't go back in time and undo what I did in college. But I would appreciate not having to hear about it all the time.

8:36pm

JAKE: When I was little I had a friend named Echo In the Dawn Mist

8:37pm

PADRAIC: I went to college with a girl named Lasagna.

8:38am

MICHAEL: \

Um...my daughter typed that. I hope that didn't break a Daddy Drinks rule or something.

8:46am

HENRY: You're out, lanahan.

#babylaw

8:47am

PADRAIC: But now that you're out- you got drugs? I know a guy who'll blow you for them.

NAPS

7:52am

MICHAEL: Question for my Daddies of older children: How old was your lovely child when they went down to one nap a day? Did they do it naturally or did you need to push & twist them in to it? And what tends to be their daytime nap schedule? We gotta crack this fucking nut.

7:55am

HENRY: Cracking your nut is how you got in this mess, I believe.

8:47am

JAKE: Blue made the switch on her own, at about 1 year.

8:48am

PADRAIC: I don't quite remember when it happened, but Freddy did it naturally- he just stopped wanting his first nap. So he had been doing 90 minutes late morning and 90 minutes early afternoon, and then he went to 3 hours in the afternoon. One of us naps with him, which means we sleep for the first 30 minutes and then get up

8:50am

JAKE: Now she's 1-3 hours once a day, somewhat random timing.

8:50am

PADRAIC: Semele and Freddy are on the same schedule!

9:22am

MICHAEL: At our 1-year appointment the doctor indicated she should go down to one nap, Right now, it's 11-1, but the next 7.5 hours until bedtime is tough. Trying to rethink our approach.

9:56am

VICTOR: Alex just stopped taking a morning nap when he didn't want it anymore. We just stopped putting him down when he stopped being sleepy. It was around the 1 year mark, but it's a little convoluted for us, because when he started going to day care, he wouldn't take a morning nap. Only on the weekends, when he was home with us.

10:09am

MICHAEL: At Alex's daycare, do they have one "naptime" for all the kids generally, or is it broken up by individuals, or age-groups? I think we'd like to start getting her into a Day-care friendly pattern…

10:17am

VICTOR: They have a specific nap time.

He was taking naps in the morning everyday at home and it immediately stopped once he started daycare

10:42am

MICHAEL: Probably all the stimulation he was getting being in that environment and around all those other kids.

11:13am

PADRAIC: I bet Alex never takes naps alone, that womanizing rascal!

11:17am

HENRY: Speaking of stimulation.

11:18am

FRENCH: He's a baby, Padraic. Albeit an extremely sexy, Billy D Williams style baby.

11:21am

HENRY: That baby is Lando Calrisian FO SHO.

TEETHING

6:22pm

HENRY: Wow. Guess what you don't want your baby to start to do before other babies?

6:53pm

PADRAIC: Using weapons.

6:58pm

HENRY: Teething. Wow.
Solid hour of screaming. Tips???

7:03pm

PADRAIC: I'm not the one to ask- Freddy had pretty uneventful teething

---

7:21pm

HENRY: I suppose it could be worse-- an hour isn't that bad, and I'm exaggerating a little bit about the non-stop screaming, but it just broke our hearts. She's barely even three months old seems very early for this.

7:44pm

MICHAEL: This isn't to say that the teeth are going to break through any time soon, or that this will now be a constant for you, but the process of those teeth slowly making their way up the gums from deep below can begin this early. At this point I don't know of a solution. Once they get closer to the surface and the pain is more acute, you can use a baby oragel (or a similar "natural" solution). Also, if she's running a fever as a result, and she's old enough, there's always children's tylenol.

8:06pm

JAKE: Ice cube in a sock... a clean sock...

7:13am

MICHAEL: Padraic: You've got an older kid, do they really need all these teeth that they have to grow? I mean, enough already.

7:14am

HENRY: Do they just lose their minds 24/7 when they're teething? I'm scared. Seriously every time she touches her face or gnaws her hand I'm like "crud."

7:15am

FRENCH: Mike, I do not believe a baby needs teeth.

7:15am

HENRY: ps when we were kids they called that salve "whiskey." It was slathered liberally on all baby's gums.

I'd chew my baby's food and spit it baby bird style to get 8 hours straight sleep.

7:17am

FRENCH: A baby doesn't eat steak, so... Why the teeth?

7:20am

HENRY: My baby better eat steak at the first sign of teething. Period.

8:02am

JAKE: For the last few days all Blue will eat is apples and milk. She's cutting canines. I guess the apples feel good on her gums. So she gets hungry hourly but won't eat a meal, won't sleep through the night because she's hungry, and poops 4 times a day. It's a good thing they're so adorable.

8:09am

MICHAEL: Sorry I had to step away for a few minutes to wipe poop out of a baby vagina, What'd I miss?

8:16am

VICTOR: Last night I was in bed at 10 o'clock. That's right 10 PM. Actually I'd been in bed since about 8 o'clock after a wicked long week I was tired so me and the wife laid in bed after putting Alex down and for a couple of hours we watch a couple shows. Daddy was falling asleep during the second show so we called it quits turned off the TV and went to sleep. For about five minutes.

8:18am

MICHAEL: Oh man, that sounds so wonderful. Right up until that last sentence.

8:19am

FRENCH: It started perfect . And then....

8:19am

VICTOR: Then the distinguished gentleman of Burbank pulls out all the stops and starts screaming bloody murder, because his teeth hurt. Cut to 2 1/2 hours later, we finally get him back down. I said to my wife as I was drifting off to sleep "Maybe he'll sleep until 8." Cut to 6am. Crying. First the kid. Then me. Whiskey, you say?

8:23am

FRENCH: They are beautiful treasures. But fuck, man.

8:27am

VICTOR: And that was the first time I'd been in bed that early in weeks. I was thinking "Finally! I'll get some rest before I'm on morning duty."

Nope!

8:30am

VICTOR: Granted, I complain, but then there are moments like this.

4:24am

FRENCH: Question for The Tooth Fairies-- We had two teeth below followed by two above. Where do the next ones show up?

7:25am

JAKE: We got more up top, but top took the lead all the way through for Blue.

7:43am

MICHAEL: The next two for us were on top on either side of the two-front teeth. Then the same on the bottom. Now...molars. Godforsaken, screaming, awful molars.

7:45am

JAKE: 😬

7:46am

JAKE: Blue has been chewing on furniture lately, like a terrier or something.

8:47am

HENRY: Dear God.

8:47am

MICHAEL: Don't worry Hank, you got a couple months...

8:58am

FRENCH: Yeah. Teeth are the worst. And it turns a simple diaper change into a judo match.

9:06am

PADRAIC: Freddy got teeth on his legs and he rubs them at night like a cricket.

9:55am

FRENCH: All I know is that I put my thumb in her mouth so she could chomp a little and she bit the living fuck outta me. And then she bit my thigh.

10:08am

VICTOR: Alex has been doing diaper change judo for almost a year now. It's gotten better, but still, if you mention diaper change, he gets this look in his eyes like "you won't best me this time, Father. This time I will prevail!" And it becomes a two person job, me holding him down while, Cindy changes the diaper, trying to not let the poop go flying through the air...again. Then as soon as it's over, he's like "wassup, guys?" As if nothing ever happened. Jerk.

10:09am

VICTOR: Also, two top, the two bottom, two more top and then a hell of a long time passed and just now he's starting to get his third on the bottom.

8:41am

PADRAIC: I woke up to this sentence: "Can you clean the poop out of Freddy's undies? I have to take a shower." Now, when a three year old shits his buzz light year undies and then runs around the house playing, it looks like Van Gogh just painted Starry Night on a small ham. And the only color he had was brown. And he used shit.

8:42am

PADRAIC: But hang in there gentlemen! They will start sleeping like regular people soon!

9:13am

VICTOR: 👍

PLEASE, PLEASE, PLEASE SLEEP.

VICTOR: Alex has started sleeping like he's from the 18th century. He sleeps for like 4 hours then gets up and wants to play and eat for an hour before going back to sleep. It's seriously fucked up!

4:16pm

MICHAEL: I recommend a whiskey salve. For him, but also for you.

5:51pm

JAKE: We hit a rough patch around 18mos... lasted a few months, but we're through it now...

Though she never really got all the way up... just needed milk…

5:59pm

VICTOR: He gets all the way up! In the beginning we just thought he was hungry or had a nightmare or something, but no. He's up and happy and not going back to bed for nothing.

6:08pm

JAKE: Brutal.

6:08pm

9:05pm

HENRY: Ouch.

10:22pm

MICHAEL: Just when you think you're out, they pull you back in.

10:24pm

PADRAIC: Give him a quill and ink- he may be a time traveller.

The Quiet Hug, Part Two

PADRAIC: Freddy got his Hep and Polio shots today. So we are finally all good to experience the joy that is Nigerian Sex Tourism.

FRENCH: It's a "package deal."

JAKE: Take a nap, French.

PADRAIC: I want a nap too.

VICTOR: That's what I told Cindy. "I've got a package deal for you. Here's my package, deal with it."

JAKE: Chapter title: Romantic Conception Stories

PADRAIC: It all started that fateful day when Alex Isaac pulled up on his tricycle and said he was there to give my wife "a ride."

12:40pm

VICTOR: 👍

12:49pm

JAKE: I was leaving town, and Crystal had determined that her moon was full, so we had this high-pressure, marathon session in the shower... it completely turned it into a chore...

1:14pm

MICHAEL: ☹

1:16pm

JAKE: ... a week later I got layed off, and told her we had to stop trying...

1:17pm

FRENCH: Also- We had tried to have a baby for several years. My mother finally said "Just relax and love your wife."

And then she had a stroke. We went to visit her and it was a tough week.

It was there we had "the quiet hug." In my childhood bedroom. My mother was right.

11:24pm

JAKE: 🐱

12:08am

JAKE: That fat kitty seems kinda smart-assy, but it really is pretty nice, the loving thing...

12:09pm

FRENCH: See? Sidney gets it.

12:11pm

PADRAIC: The best sex we ever had was in a sleeping bag in the basement of her sisters house during the holidays. We had to be quiet and we couldn't see anything. Like how moles do it, I would assume.

1:11am

1:12am

HENRY: Checking that.

Yep, confirmed. That's how moles do.

Also would have accepted "in the butt."

As an answer. Not sexually from you, padraic.

Quiet hug is incredible in mom-in-law's basement every Christmas. Sweet and epic every time.

1:15am

FRENCH: It's occasionally "hand over the loud mouth sex." Which is good.

1:16am

HENRY: I've had that once. It's naughty. And thrilling!

1:17am

FRENCH: Oh it's filthy.

1:18am

HENRY: She knows she needs to be quiet and you know she's not gonna be quiet.

1:18am

PADRAIC: Then you gotta clean up, and the bathroom is always on the third floor past the bedroom where the cousins are sleeping.

And the floor creaks.

1:20am

HENRY: Ma-in-law's basement has a converted terlet!! Luxury!!! I walk around naked down there every visit like a king! A naked king.

1:21am

FRENCH: The Quiet Hug is Baby Law.

1:22am

HENRY: Baby Law.

1:22am

PADRAIC: I love you guys.

1:22am

HENRY: This means the world to me.

Also that's what I say before trotting my naked bod around MaryLou's basement.

FRENCH: Daddy hug
1:23am

HENRY: I wear slippers. I'm not a hobo.
I miss you dudes. This makes the missing less. And it's a sweet new level to my already existing love for each of you scoundrels.
1:23am

FRENCH: "I wear slippers. I'm not a hobo."
That's right.
1:25am

PADRAIC: Btw, I got two days of solo daddy this week- Emily's out of town. So send good baby law vibes my way...
1:27am

HENRY: Sending. Lanahan, get in here with some support, man!!
Baby Law power. ACTIVATE.
1:27am

MICHAEL: Sorry, Gents, the wife had overnight/early shift. *yaaaawn*
1. Oh, man. Had an incredible hand-over-themouth Quiet Hug, at the old homestead several years ago. Same place I had all my high school make-out sessions. Epic.
2. Padraic, I can tell you from experience that nothing helps fill that time without the wife like Quietly Hugging oneself....at least two or three times per day. BABY LAW POWER!
9:38am

MICHAEL: (Also, if you're looking to kill/fill time, come on down to the South Bay! Love to have ya!)
9:40am

VICTOR: I never get to do the quiet hug at someone else's house. Cindy gets all self conscious about it. The only time we do the quiet hug is when my mother visits. She sleeps in the living room which is on the other side of our bedroom wall, so we gots to keep it quiet. The only other time was when Alex was sleeping in the bed. Then it's the slow-mo quiet hug, because you don't want the bed to jiggle too much.
11:01am

11:02am

HENRY: Padraic ? Michael is inviting you to come down to the south bay for a tandem solo quiet hug. Either go for it or be careful, but you've been warned

11:09am

MICHAEL: The South Bay is for Lovers. Quiet. Solo. Lovers.

(After all, I had to go the the Dominican Republic to get this baby conceived!)

11:41am

JAKE: Finley is Dominican? Awesome.

11:42am

MICHAEL: Anchor Baby.

THE MONEY PROBLEM

3:15pm

MICHAEL: Just an interjection: The neighbor came over because she wanted to grab Finley and play - and it's incredible how fast the recall is to it just being Angela & I. We were running around doing stuff, talking and there was an instant 5 minutes where it was over a year ago and just us. So mind-blowing.

3:28pm

VICTOR: ...someone came and took your baby? What's that like?

I mentioned to Cindy the other day that we need to find someone we could trust to leave Alex overnight and she almost got teary eyed and said, "Not yet."

3:31pm

JAKE: We send her on vacations with Grampy twice a month, 3-4 nights... That's when we catch up on the dishes and laundry!

3:33pm

HENRY: Please tell me that dishes and laundry are code for sex and drinking. Otherwise I have no hope.

MICHAEL: I think I feel bad that that instant felt like a wonderful, albeit temporary, relief.

3:36pm

FRENCH: Vanessa's mother will Take Helene for 4 nights. We sleep, have sex one or twice and look at pictures she sends of the baby. Then once we're home it's almost instantly back to the grind.

3:38pm

HENRY: sex once or TWICE???? luxury!!!

3:59pm

VICTOR: Twice a month!!???!!!
Holy cow! That's awesome!
And you shouldn't feel bad, Lanahan. This shit is hard work 24/7. Shit, if you can get an hour break with your wife, and not talk about the kid, that's pretty awesome.

4:00pm

PADRAIC: I had no idea everyone has been having regular baby vacations. Since Freddy was born, I think I've

4:11pm

only been away from him for about a week.
Jake- you're saying Grampy has the baby 3-4 nights twice a month? So 8 days a month? That's more like a time share baby.

JAKE: pretty much all we did for 8 years was drink and fuck, so we've got a lot of catching up to do...

4:26pm

HENRY: Fucking A

4:39pm

JAKE: Yeah, that was a joke... the truth is we're both partially employed independent contractors who barely make enough money each week... when she goes to the grandparents we can both work 8-hour days through the weekend, catch up on the household chores, and occasionally see a play... and they're happy to have her... I miss her terribly every time...

9:44pm

HENRY: Dude I'm sure. Don't forget sleep. I'm sure it's great for your sanity. Much love, jake.
Much love all, my Drunken Daddies.

10:23pm

PADRAIC: Jake- I hear ya. We're in the same boat. You need free time to make money, but you need money to make that free time. We should all just dump our kids at one of our houses each day and let everyone else have a break.

10:27pm

JAKE: Yeah, 1 dad with 6 kids... Good plan...

10:28pm

HENRY: (Dittman fear pukes)

10:30pm

JAKE: Don't worry Hank, I'm pretty sure Padraic volunteered to be first...

10:31pm

MICHAEL: I'm new into this boat myself. I'm trying to figure out how we can both hustle some jobs now, while being able to find someplace to stash our kid in the meantime. It's past time Gramma and Grampa get that room ready for their grand-daughter.

10:31pm

JAKE: My mother is moving to Los Angeles...

10:32pm

PADRAIC: And into my house! (there was a time that would have been a mom joke about sex, but now I just wish an older lady would move in to my house and take care of my kid.)

10:35pm

HENRY: Sarah started auditioning again last week and so far it's worked. But it's taken some juggling. Nervy stuff...

10:36pm

MICHAEL: Just so you guys know (cuz you're my Daddies, and you're who I can talk to), Angela just got laid off after 7 years, so we're kinda scrambling right now. Just corporate down-sizing, but we've never really had to scramble like this before (a luxury, I know). I'm a bit nervous, but there's a kid now, so whatever has to be done, has to be done. I'm really ready to set some of her former employers on fire, but it's for the best - she was miserable. Deep, cleansing breaths....right?

10:36pm

10:37pm

HENRY: She's gonna find something quick, brother. And your big gig is just about to happen. Believe it.

Sorry you guys are going through that mike.

10:39pm

PADRAIC: I'm with Henry on this- something great is gonna smack you in the face. it's baby law.

10:40pm

MICHAEL: It's so strange, and so "adult" when this shit happens and you've got a baby. The responsibility is so motivating and scary.

10:40pm

HENRY: That's what padraic said to emily on their wedding night as well.

10:40pm

MICHAEL: 😄

10:41pm

HENRY: Absolutely mike. Everyone said I wouldn't care about auditions when the baby came. I care so much more. It affects me less personally. But they mean more.

10:50pm

PADRAIC: I feel the exact same way! I have never felt more motivated, and I have never had less time to act on it.

11:04pm

MICHAEL: I try not to weigh down auditions with too much meaning or, "desperation" especially. But now I'm not so much trying to build a resume as build steady work. I feel like before I was in it for me and my wife, and for some glory. Now I'm just trying to provide. Fatherhood just shifted into second gear, y'know?

11:06pm

HENRY: You got this mike.

11:09pm

MICHAEL:

11:09pm

HENRY: Put that tongue back in your mouth mister. And the thumb needs holstering as well.

11:10pm

FRENCH: When Vanessa got pregnant it was sort of a mixed shock. My last sperm actually had dog paddled his way to victory - and I was pretty washed up and running out of money. But my mind shifted. And a job came. Nobody was more surprised than me.

11:31pm

MICHAEL: Alright, gents. Thanks for the ears tonight - I'm on duty until 7am, so I'm going to try to sleep whilst I'm able. Cheers, and good luck to all through the night-shifts.

11:31pm

FRENCH: I love you. Mike. Go sleep.

BABIES ARE DICKS

6:41am

FRENCH: Good morning. It looks like Willy Wonka has been experimenting in Helene's Diaper.

7:16am

MICHAEL: Lessons learned in retrospect: If you've got a big callback the next morning, go to bed extra early, because that's the morning your baby will choose to wake up screaming at dawn like a total shit. #babylaw

7:20am

FRENCH: I like going in front of a live studio audience after someone decided to birth teeth. Like an ass hole.

7:24am

MICHAEL: It's clear to me now that our babies hate our careers and want us to fail.

7:29am

FRENCH: It's almost like college doesn't matter.

7:30am

MICHAEL: Or food, or clothes, or medicine.

8:06pm

MICHAEL: After a difficult couple days in BabyTown, Angela: "Our baby is such a dick. Why is our baby such a dick?"

11:10pm

FRENCH: Just today I referred to the baby as acting like a short little dick. Toddlers are sociopaths.

12:55pm

VICTOR: Tell me about it.

Alex screams that he's hungry, but then screams when he has to sit down to eat, then screams when you give him food. WHO IS THIS ALIEN IN MY HOUSE!

8:28pm

FRENCH: I am now open to putting the baby in a local bird nest to see if they would take to her. Or giving her to a barren couple.

9:22pm

MICHAEL: I tried to leave leave Finley in the produce section yesterday, hoping some festive couple might take her for a novelty screaming pumpkin.

The grocery manager chased after me laughing at the "hilarious joke" I just pulled. *sigh*

8:59pm

JAKE: Blue has discovered a powerful new improv technique... We call it: "No, and?"

9:59am

FRENCH: Helene picked something up off the floor and put it in her mouth. I pulled it out and realized it was a cracker. So I put it back in her mouth. Then I remembered it had been sitting on the floor and I pulled it out. Now she looks at me like I'm fucking with her. So I put it back in her mouth. Terrible decision making today.

10:05am

MICHAEL: I think a good parent would then tell her you love her more than anything, and then sweep the legs out from under her.

3:31pm

JAKE: Comedy is based on suffering. They have to start sometime.

9:26pm

VICTOR: Is 17 1/2 months too soon to start terrorizing your child with a water hose? To be fair, he was asking for it.

Asking for a friend.

10:44pm

MICHAEL: Oh I've met Ale-...er, your friends kid. And he's asking for it.

7:36am

MICHAEL: Oooh! Willy Wonka just arrived! 👍

7:38am

FRENCH:

Taking Care of Other Peoples' Kids

7:42am

PADRAIC: For the next four hours, I'm in charge of two kids. #myfuture #ijustwanttodrinkcoffeeinsilence

7:46am

MICHAEL: You've got one on the way, and now you're adopting?! STOP!

7:48am

HENRY: No no, KEEP GOING, padraic! Take all of ours for the day!!!!!

7:49am

FRENCH: Operation Dumbo Drop.

7:51am

HENRY: Gumbo Drop.

7:52am

FRENCH: Frumbo Frop

7:55am

HENRY: Bingo

7:56am

FRENCH: Yahtzee...Why is this happening?

8:07am

PADRAIC: Freddy's 4 year old cousin is visiting with his mom. I'm stuck with the kids until noon! They tandem pooed just now: Freddy in his undies, and his cousin on the potty. Im double hand wiping! Now I'm pooping! Poops everywhere, guys. It's getting scary.

8:12am

FRENCH: I'm also Fedexing you my poop.

8:12am

PADRAIC: I won't sign for it! I won't!

8:14am

FRENCH: I've asked them to leave it on the porch. And light it on fire.

8:36am

PADRAIC: I just signed for it. I opened it. It's full of poop.

8:37am

FRENCH: Fire poop?

8:37am

MICHAEL: *sigh* Padraic I'm starting to think you bring this all on yourself.

8:41am

HENRY: I'm boxing up our dye-ah-pur pail now.

8:50am

PADRAIC: And it was at this moment that Padraic had reached...The Pooping Point.

8:55am

FRENCH: The Pooping Point. By John Grisham?

8:57am

MICHAEL: Unrelated question: Can I get your address, Padraic?

THE POOPING POINT

MICHAEL: "It was a dark, and stormy evening when the poop started arriving at my doorstep. Package after package of poop…"

FRENCH: I can't believe that The Pooping Point by John Grisham gets it's own chapter.

VICTOR: He slowly came to, his head pounding. He tried to move and discovered his hands were gagged and bound, laying on some crappy shag carpet fresh out of an episode of "The Brady Bunch." "If, I had a nickel…" he thought as he tried to sit up. BANG! Half way to sitting his head smashed into what was apparently the bottom of a glass coffee table. "For fucks sake!" he muffled through the gag as stars exploded in his eyes. He blinked furiously to clear his vision as the figure of a woman peered down at him through the glass. "You're awake," she casually said, as if he'd fallen asleep on the couch during an episode of "Revolution" and woke up during the 11 o'clock news. She reached underneath the table and pulled the gag down so he could speak freely. "Who the hell puts a sleeping person underneath a glass table.!?!?" "Who the hell follows a lady into an alley?" "Oh, that was you. Sorry, you didn't look like a lady." "You don't look like a man." He was lying, he had no doubt she was a lady when he followed her into the alley, but he had questions and figured she had the answers. And even though he was tied up, he still needed those answers. "So, how do you know the Wolf?" "Ha! Sorry, Francis, I'm going to be the one asking questions. And I hope you have the answers." She unbuttoned her pants and slid her pants and panties down to her ankles before stepping out of them. "Hey lady, if you're trying to get answers out of me, you're doing it wrong." She walked over to the table, picked up a pack of cigarettes and a lighter and studied his face as she shook a cigarette out before putting it in her mouth and lighting it. "I'm just saying, it's been a long time, so I may not last as long. Also, I should warn you, I have herpes and I like to share." "You're very funny, Francis." "You should see me do a set at Flapper's" "OK, first question. What's the square root of 3,627,582" she asked, as she stepped onto the glass coffee table. What the fuck was she talking about? "What the fuck are you talking about?" "Don't know?" "No, I don't know. I failed algebra." She squatted over him. "Welcome to Cleveland!" she exclaimed with a delighted glee. "Lady, I hate to break it to you, but we aren't in...." And it was at that point he realized he'd found "The Pooping Point."

12:29pm

FRENCH: (Super slow) Clap...clap....Clap

WHY WE DO IT

MICHAEL: In a rare display of gushing love for my child, it's breaking my fucking heart-hole that Finley is getting too big to wear on my chest in the Bjorn, and too big to be in the car seat stroller attachment. Now when I take her out she's facing away from me and we can't look at each other anymore. *sigh*

VICTOR: I know the feeling. When Alex was just a wee lad and being fussy at night, I'd strap him on and walk up and down the street with him until he fell asleep. I miss those times.

HENRY: The cure all for Hannah's fussing is sitting in my hand leaned on my chest facing outward, particularly as we walk around the yard. We're Basque, so I'm pretty sure she gets overheated like daddy. I can't wait to talk with her and walk with her but those twilights are so precious. I'm gonna miss 'em when they're gone.

MICHAEL: By that same token, she's finally reached a point that sometimes when I hold her she'll bury/nuzzle her head on my shoulder and neck - which she never did before. And then time stops.

JAKE: Aww. You'll laugh about the hard times someday. That day might be in the 2030s or so, but it will come... I'm pretty sure... No, it will, I know it…

12:30am

PADRAIC: Freddy just said to me "I'm starting to grow up like Daddy." He's trying to make me cry, right?

1:21pm

MICHAEL: I don't...there just...some dust landed in my eye, that's all. Geez! *sniff*

1:21pm

VICTOR: Aww...jeez…

2:51pm

FRENCH: I hate when I have to toss out 8 solid jokes because of an actually nice moment.

2:57pm

JAKE: Just copy them to a document and paste them in randomly…

4:02pm

MICHAEL: This weekend, we took her out to the pier in the bike trailer. It was incredible and so special. And her blank stare through a mesh window while wearing an over-sized baby helmet made the cherry on top. Great weekend. This is really becoming next-level enjoyable.

10:52pm

MICHAEL:

10:52pm

8:19am
JAKE: That's great, Mike... The payoff continues! Baby bike time on the beach this summer!

9:09am
HENRY: So happy for you mike. I know it's been a tough haul for you guys and I'm glad it's improving. Mommy being home more can't hurt??!!

10:39am
MICHAEL: So far, so great.

6:04pm
HENRY: Today my daughter laughed with me. A big belly laugh. Holy crap. I get it.

6:17pm
VICTOR: Belly laughs are the best!!!

6:46pm
MICHAEL: That's it. That's the whole Universe entirely.

6:48pm
JAKE: Yep.

6:58pm
FRENCH: Also enjoy that gummy smile while you can.

7:00pm
HENRY: Oh boy it's incredible. Today first laugh while awake (she sleep laughs a lot Sarah says).

12:24am
PADRAIC: The other day Freddy said he wanted to be a writer "like Daddy." It's hard to explain to your kid that your tears are because you're happy.

12:25am
JAKE: There are so many mean things to say to that, but I don't actually want to say them... fatherhood is making me weak...

12:26am
PADRAIC: I hope he's a writer "like someone successful," ...

12:27am
JAKE: Yeah, see? It's so easy that it's kind of unsatisfying...

12:27am

PADRAIC: Like your mom.

12:27am

JAKE:

12:28am

PADRAIC: Fried egg man is upset.

8:43am

MICHAEL: If my daughter tells me she wants to be an actress, I'll full on punch her in the heart.

SEPARATION ANXIETY

9:51am

JAKE: Blue gets sad when I leave for work. This morning she put on her hat and grabbed her shoes so she could come with me. I had to point out that she wasn't wearing any pants.

10:00am

VICTOR: Alex has started getting upset when we leave to go to daycare. When he knows we're getting close to leaving, he will sometimes grab a book and bring it over to me. When I take it from him, he goes over to the rocker and looks back at me. I have no choice but to sit down, pull him onto my lap and read "Mr. Brown Can Moo! Can you?" twelve times in a row.

10:24am

JAKE: 👍

10:54am

MICHAEL: 👍
I also know for a fact that Mr. Brown CAN moo. That fucker moos with the best of 'em.

11:37am

JAKE: I want a personal penguin.

BEDTIME RITUALS

FRENCH: We have a sleep ritual that doesn't change. A sink bath, lotion with mommy, bottle with daddy. It lets her know it's time for the "long dark nap " not the "short bright nap."

Then daddy has lotion time with mommy.

VICTOR: Yeah, when you get to the point when she's sleeping a good chunk, sleep rituals are a MUST!

FRENCH: But in the first few months is all taking shifts and general grabassery.

MICHAEL: We've also had a set night-time ritual since she was 1 month old. Boob, bath, swaddle/pajamas, bed. This kind of routine will also cue her in to learning day vs. night. Stupid babies. They don't even know day from night.

FRENCH: And every time you get cocky with your routine, someone cuts a tooth or grows an inch. Then it's back to fuckville.

2:16pm

HENRY: Loud and clear on routines. Takes a lot of pressure off!!! We're trying the pack n play bassinet tonight and shifts!!!

2:19pm

HENRY: Today my daughter reached out and touched something that I put in front of her face. First time doing that. She also has been legitimately recognizing me and giggling and smiling, and when I hold her in my arms and sing to her she just goes gaga. Suddenly everything is fucking worth it.

BABYPROOFING

FRENCH: I'm at my mom's house. The baby found a very large bobby pin and tried to "Kobayashi" it like a hotdog. Fast hands save the day.

MICHAEL: Oh man, you are officially in the watch-for-everything-she-puts-in-her-damn-mouth stage. I'm told that won't end for another 18 years. Godspeed to your lightening reflexes, sir.

FRENCH: Once I was emptying the dishwasher while she was playing bowl & spoon and turned around in time to see her wielding a steak knife.

MICHAEL: 🙂

FRENCH: Up until tonight, Helene had only put together a few steps. Today she is walking like a person who walks in walkathons. Anybody?

JAKE: No more relaxing in front of NFL Network for French!

10:14pm

FRENCH: It's absolute pride. And terror.

10:19pm

MICHAEL: The more you baby-proof, the more you can sit back and let her wander while you kick back and watch Real Housewives of Atlanta. I'm assuming.

10:23pm

FRENCH: I love getting practical advice.

10:27pm

MICHAEL: I'm just looking out for your ability to watch TV and drink whiskey. This is paramount.

10:28pm

MICHAEL: Here's your new house rule: measure how high she can reach now walking. Everything in the house from that height on down is fair game.

10:36pm

PADRAIC: You are entering the period of babyhood that almost killed Lanahan and me. Good news? You get through it!

Practical advice tip #1: secure you dressers to the wall. Your kid will soon try to open every drawer, and it only takes 3 or 4 open drawers for the weight to shift and the whole dresser falls on your kid.

10:46pm

MICHAEL: Practical advice tip #2: The word "No" is probably about to become more common and repetitive. This is when they begin to learn boundaries.

10:56pm

PADRAIC: #3: playing with your kid is going to often be mind-numbingly, soul-crushingly, eyes-liquefyingly boring. Don't feel guilty if you feel that way. It's normal. As long as you don't lock her in the clothes hamper and drive to a bar, you're doing alright.

10:59pm

MICHAEL: On the other hand, it'll be incredibly exciting for her to walk to a wall and pat it, and then walk to a cabinet and touch the drawer knob, so... pretty easy, entertainment-wise.

11:01pm

11:17pm

PADRAIC: But then she will try to put the drawer knob in her nose. If she's gonna have a minor fall - let her. A big fall? Catch her. And the whiter the shirt you're wearing, the more they will bleed on you.

But most of it is fun! ☺

12:51am

JAKE: #4: Either you or your wife will expect your child to start learning boundaries... the spouse that puts less of a timetable on that will have to learn to be as patient with the other spouse as they are with the baby...

4:52am

HENRY: We got a tooth poking though and a baby clearly about to start scooting if not crawling. I'm terrified.

6:53am

FRENCH: I miss the toothless, gummy smiles. And the lack of movement.

8:16am

MICHAEL: #babylaw

8:17am

FRENCH: Baby Law.

8:19am

HENRY: For real.

8:21am

PADRAIC: Good thing I get to do all of that over again! (The playwright cries silently, his friends unaware except for him stating it in the stage directions)

8:22am

HENRY: You're so lucky !!!!!(pitying head shakes all around)

8:28am

FRENCH: Congrats Padraic! (Confused expression for dude who fell for it twice)

9:09am

JAKE: Won't it be great when we're all having Daddy and Me beach days and Paddy is stuck at home with an infant?

9:34am

HENRY: Won't it be wonderful when our kids are making extra money by babysitting his fifth baby?

10:24am

JAKE: Won't it be awesome when we're hiring 10-year-old Freddy for manual labor so he can help support his family?

10:47am

PADRAIC: Freddy's special skills include: dancing like a crazy person, finding the iPad no matter where we hide it, and making sure the first act of any pee pee session is in the undies and not the toilet.

12:29pm

FRENCH: You need to watch Freddy putting his finger in an open plug. With a fork.

Crap. Helene just ate a lump of Polio. Thanks.

12:35pm

JAKE: I don't want to judge, French, but you probably shouldn't have lumps of Polio just lying around...

12:35pm

PADRAIC: It's better than a smear of AIDS.

12:39pm

FRENCH: Both are fun size.

12:39pm

JAKE: I hear that's good on a Rosemary-Olive Oil Triscuit...

12:39pm

HENRY: Why not smear the aids on the polio lump? I mean they're both right there.

12:40pm

JAKE: I knew we were approaching Dittman-level...

FRENCH STEWART WANTS TO HAVE SEX WITH OUR WIVES

6:20pm

FRENCH: I've been a little down and was wondering if I could make love to each of your wives? Nothing emotional.

Just meat play.

6:31pm

JAKE: Reason #75 to remain unmarried…

6:34pm

HENRY: You know, French, Sarah deserves to be happy. Why not?

10:50pm

MICHAEL: Can I watch? Nothing gay.

Just want to learn how its done.

12:56am

PADRAIC: French - tell me what it's like.

10:03am

VICTOR: Speaking of old ladies, your moms wanted me to tell you hi and that they are satisfied.

I'm implying that I've slept with your moms.

SWADDLING

HENRY: Hey guys, we are at about three months and three weeks and Hannah has been flipping from her back to her front like crazy the last few days. We sleep her in a swaddle, actually in a sleep pod called a Woombie. We're nervous about her rolling over onto her face in her sleep and not being able to roll back over because of the swaddle, but she needs the swaddle to sleep. When did you guys stop swaddling? Any thoughts on this in general? We worry she's too young for us to sleep train her, but I'm open to any advice from you fellas. Help!!!

8:38pm

MICHAEL: Our transition was the one-arm, then two-arm free swaddle. I believe he illustrates it in Happiest Baby. After that, there's really nothing else but putting her in the footie pajamas and letting her sleep arms and legs akimbo (No blanket yet). It may take a night or three for her to get used to it, but there's no "sleep training" to help her adjust to being out of the swaddle - she's just gotta get used to it. It may also create a new night-time sleep schedule, as she adjusts to being free, & waking herself up with flailing limbs.

11:19pm

MICHAEL: Don't worry about her suffocating - if she has the strength to roll herself over, then she has the strength to lift herself and shift her head when sleeping.

Just make sure it's just her in the crib and nothing else she could roll onto (i.e. blanket, stuffed animal) and suffocate from. Once she could roll-over, Finley was a total tummy sleeper. Still is. It's fucking adorable.

PADRAIC: Freddy loved to sleep on his stomach. Made me very nervous.

We did the one arm free for a long time. We called it a "light swaddle," which meant that we tucked the blanket under him snugly, but that he could wriggle his arms free if he tried. So that gave him some comfort, but it also made us feel better about him possibly flipping over, which he started doing at around 3 or 4 months. And my wife says that they have just put out new guidelines about swaddling- that they are recommending that it not be as tight.

VICTOR: I echo Lanahan. If she has the strength to roll over, she has the strength to lift her head when necessary. Though making sure there's nothing else she can roll onto would be good as well. After the swaddle, we co-slept, and Alex still slept on his back, after we transitioned him to the crib, he immediately became a stomach sleeper. He still is. When we put him down, he gathers up the small blanket in his crib and puts it under his stomach and sleeps with his butt in the air.

PADRAIC: Then when they are 3, they begin to sleep in the craziest positions possible. The other day for his nap he slept with a two foot plastic buzz lightyear under his butt - every time he moved, I would hear from the other room "Hi, I'm Buzz Lightyear!"

HENRY: Butt Lightrear.

HENRY: Also "Does TightRear."
Also thanks for the support boys!
Does TightRear. C'mon. That's nice.

PADRAIC: Fuzz bite smear.

HENRY: Yes!

VICTOR: Alex didn't turn over until almost 6 months. I don't think it's possible to turn over while she's in the swaddle. I don't think...

7:52pm

FRENCH: Helene flipped around 6 months too. I stared at the baby monitor the whole time.

8:08pm

PADRAIC: It's crazy how quickly your forget the milestones.

10:22pm

JAKE: 6 months seems about right, but I echo Padraic: it fades so fast... there was also a phase where she was swaddled to get to sleep, but would work her way out... once the swaddle went away for good, Blue would immediately flip into this crazy arch on her side: the exact position she had in the womb... I spent a few weeks gently rolling her onto her back, but she would snap back every time like she was spring-loaded... by then she could push herself up and fall over to the side, so we figured she was as safe as she could be...

12:09am

MICHAEL: Finley flipped around 4 months - she was real early with it. but I know EXACTLY what you're dealing with Henry. We had the same problem. What we did was roll up a little towel length-wise and put them on either side of her in the crib. That way she wouldn't roll over in her sleep while swaddled. When she's ready to get out of the swaddle, I think you'll know by the way she constantly breaks out of it (at least, that was our cue).

1:54am

FRENCH: Do you have a nail gun?

2:10am

HENRY: Yes. Yes I do. It's a finishing nail gun so the nails are smaller. Baby-size?

I Call My Penis "Henry Wrinkler"

PADRAIC: Any of you guys wanna get out of the house tonight and see a play? I have two tickets to opening night of THE TALLEST TREE at the Taper, and Emily's not going…

9:19am

FRENCH: I can't. I'm going to your house to be with Emily.

Is the gang bang off?

9:40am

JAKE: ☺

9:50am

PADRAIC: If you have sex with my wife, please tell me what it's like!

Rimshot! Cry….

9:51am

JAKE: That's what it's like…

9:52am

PADRAIC: 😂

9:53am

9:55am

JAKE: Do we need to get Padraic some professional assistance?

9:58am

PADRAIC: If only a sitcom star could awaken her sexuality…

10:01am

JAKE: There's your rom-com, Paddy…

10:18am

FRENCH: I've got Henry Winkler on speed dial!

10:29am

PADRAIC: I call my penis "Henry Wrinkler."

10:39am

FRENCH: I hope your Fonzie doesn't end up in someone's Malph.

10:40am

PADRAIC: I put my Wrinkler in her Chachi.

12:49pm

FRENCH: Have you put your Pinkie Tuscadero in her Pottsie? They don't always want that.

12:59pm

JAKE: rama-lama-lama, ka-dingidy-ding-de-ding!

1:03pm

FRENCH: See. Sidney gets it.

1:08pm

HENRY: Strong work fellas.
Emily deserves to be happy.

2:47pm

FRENCH: Why is everybody suddenly being so disrespectful to Paddy and his wife?

3:34pm

HENRY: I think it's Incredibly respectful.

3:37pm

FRENCH: You might be right, Ditty. Well, off to the Dildo Store.

3:50pm

FRENCH: Crap. Cake on my face. Can anyone recommend a good dildo store?

4:00pm

PADRAIC: My favorite Dildo store is "Crap Cake on my Face." It's on Wilshire.

4:00pm

HENRY: They also make great crab cakes.

4:18pm

PADRAIC: Btw, when this chapter goes in the book "Emily" will be called "McSharon Inthebutt"

4:24pm

FRENCH: Because she kept her maiden name.

5:11pm

HENRY: Of the Connecticut Inthebutts?

5:29pm

JAKE: McSharon deserves to be happy.

8:07pm

FRENCH: Just got back from the gang bang. A real disappointment. McSharon made it clear that nothing was happening. And then she gave 11 guys errands that she would like finished by Wednesday. I can't believe I have to get your car smog checked.

SWIMMING

11:27pm

MICHAEL: So today I got into the pool with my little girl for the first time ever, and it was like everything I thought and wanted fatherhood to be. It lasted all of five minutes (cuz it was kinda chilly out and her little baby bottom lip started quivering with cold), but all I want to do is live in the pool with my daughter until she's 13. Then her mother can have her. I'm telling you - like floating on a cloud of smiles and wonder.

11:27pm

MICHAEL: 😂

11:33pm

FRENCH: I love you, Mike. That's the stuff.

12:03am

JAKE: Joyous... The first time Blue and I swam she carried an expression of stunned, exhilarated joy I will remember till the day I die... it lasted until I was swimming backward, just kicking with my feet while holding her up, her looking around and gently slapping the water with peaceful amusement... and I rammed my head straight into the brick lip of the pool wall... I assumed either my mother or hers, both of whom were watching from the side, would offer some kind of warning before that happened... nope...

12:15am

FRENCH: I love that, Jake. I really love that.

12:17am

PADRAIC: The way a child holds you in the water- I have never felt more quietly needed. A trust I never will break. Btw, right now I'm drinking cheap Trader joes champagne and eating stale popcorn. Cause I'm a man.

12:21am

JAKE: 😊 OK!

12:23am

FRENCH: I've just finished a 4 pack of tiny liquor store wine.

12:25am

PADRAIC: I think of you like a mentor.

12:26am

FRENCH: That's not fortunate.

12:28am

PADRAIC: But it's fun!

12:41am

FRENCH: You fuckers.

10:47am

PADRAIC:

10:48am

PADRAIC: Here's Freddy's first swim class!

10:48am

VICTOR: 👍

10:56am

JAKE: Awesome.

6:05pm

PADRAIC: And here's Freddy's swim class this week which was canceled because someone shit in the pool. So we ate snow cones.

6:05pm

HENRY: "This swim class shit is bad ass, padraic duffy" I imagine Freddy calls you by your full name.

6:32pm

MICHAEL: Hey, that reminds me: Finley shit the tub last night for the first time! More specifically: diarrhea-ed the tub. And I was at the theater! Woo-Hoo!

6:34pm

JAKE: Well played, Daddy! Pour yourself a drink!

6:56pm

HENRY: Better yet tell Angela to pour you a drink!!!

6:57pm

MICHAEL: (I'll never be allowed to leave the house again)

NOISE MACHINES

7:16am

HENRY: Whoever made sleep sheep with a timer is the devil.

9:34am

MICHAEL: Grab a sound app on your phone or ipad - those are usually timeless.

10:04am

HENRY: Did!

10:42am

JAKE: What is this "sound app?"

11:16am

FRENCH: I just threw a talking bear in the garbage because I have fucking well heard enough.

11:48am

JAKE: Freddy gave Semele a puzzle for her 1st birthday that's a bunch of musical instruments: When you get one in the correct place, it plays Old MacDonald... the frequency is somehow sensitive to light switches, because if one of the puzzle pieces is not in its place when you turn the lights out, it triggers a midi-electro Old MacDonald from the puzzle, which is (naturally) hidden in some pile of toys somewhere in the house... it's terrifying...

2:21pm

MICHAEL: The app we used is Sleep Pillow.

We also had a sound and light up Teddy Bear that someone gave us second-hand, and it would go off on it's own. Often when lights were off, or the room was dead quiet. It went in the fucking trash like a dirty di-ah-pur!

2:40pm

FRENCH: I've found that Helene would rather play with an empty box or a Cheeto bag that anything we ever bought.

4:50pm

FRENCH: But I also believe that when Darlene steals her toy it's a lesson in sharing.

11:40pm

PADRAIC: We ripped a sound machine out of a random teddy bear.

And that sound machine was the most important item in our house for three months.

We changed diapers...to the beat of the rhythm of the night!

11:44pm

JAKE: Atwater Sound Machine

7:45am

FRENCH: My baby shakes my bottle of low dose, old man aspirin while I try to pull her leg through a pair of pants before the other one comes out.

7:45am

HENRY: They never both go in the pants.

7:50am

FRENCH: It's turned into Greco Roman wrestling.

7:51am

HENRY: Those little hamhocks move quick, little ninja kicks!

7:53am

FRENCH: Yeah. If we're both home, I pin her down and Vanessa pulls em on. But if I'm alone it's a judo match.

7:53am

HENRY: Mine is tae kwon do.

7:54am

FRENCH: Babies are as dumb as hell.

7:58am

HENRY: Not dads. Super fucking smart.

8:15am

MICHAEL: #babylaw

DADDY PHASE

> **FRENCH:** Vanessa left for NY for a day. And now BaBa (me) is back! Hugs O' Plenty! And eMama is a bag of shit.
>
> Crappy, poopy shit.
>
> Nice.
>
> The baby thinks her mom is a fart. And I'm a golden wonder. Fun. BaBa is back!
>
> *8:21pm*

> **MICHAEL:** Attention everyone: Do NOT take the brown acid. The brown acid is bad!
>
> *8:43pm*

> **FRENCH:** But it's delicious. I'm eating it. Sidney?
>
> Vic?
>
> Paddy? Mikey Moo?
>
> Me?
>
> Hanky Poo?
>
> *9:01pm*

> **VICTOR:** I'm not sure what the question is?
>
> *9:03pm*

> **FRENCH:** We dropping acid.
>
> *9:04pm*

11:35am

FRENCH: 😂

11:20pm

PADRAIC: I'm gone for a day, and this thread loses its mind

2:01am

JAKE: ☺ **hi.**

11:23pm

MICHAEL: My daughter is going through a rare I-Pre-fer-Daddy phase lately. And rather than annoying me, it's taking my breath away. What the hell is happening to me?! (Good-night, Gentlemen.)

9:16am

VICTOR: one of the best things about working is coming home. At the sound of me coming in the door Alex gets excited and as soon as he sees me he runs over to me screaming and giggling and I pick him up and give him a hug. It's one of the best things on the planet. However, just to prove that he's my son and to show he's got comedy chops, every now and again he runs over to me and when he's just about a foot out of my reach he turns around and runs towards his mom and when she scoops him up he laughs manically and looks back at me like "Psych!"

7:01am

HENRY: This cup is a litmus. 50% of the time it feels like an ironic smirk. 50% an astute encouragement. This morning we're riding the line. Leaning towards the positive.

MIKE FLIES WITH THE BABY

7:46am

MICHAEL: Tomorrow morning, we get into a pressurized tin-can with our baby and go to 30,000 feet for 5 hours. I'm...anxious. *gulp*

8:06am

HENRY: That fills me with more dread than college tuition.

8:48am

JAKE: Last summer we took 6 plane rides over two trips... She was a dream for the first five: either knocked out by the plane starting up, or a little whining on the ascent before falling asleep... On the 6th she had a stomach bug, and I was with her alone... As we were getting to our seats she puked over 4 people in three rows... I changed her in the lav while the plane was taxiing and got her to sleep... she woke up with a puke that filled our seat (she was in my lap), and I used every available wipe and extra clothing article we had... we exited reeking of sour milk... people were remarkably understanding... Good luck, Mike!

8:53am

MICHAEL: I'm considering Children's Dramamine to knock her out. Or Whiskey. Probably Whiskey.

8:56am

JAKE: It's getting from the car to the plane that's the real terror: Everything that's hard about flying times 1000…

10:53am

FRENCH: TSA treats babies like they're bombs.

11:06am

VICTOR: We flew to NYC over Xmas and I was super nervous about it. On the way there, he was an absolute angel. Not a peep. Slept a couple of hours on the way there, and was manageable the rest of the time. After we landed, he got cranky in the cab to the hotel, but I couldn't blame him.

11:07am

VICTOR: On the way home, he had a total melt down as we were getting on the plane that lasted 20 minutes. He wanted to nurse, but we needed him to wait for the ascent. It was not awesome.

11:08am

FRENCH: I got thrown up on. In my face.

11:41am

FRENCH: We had 4 connecting flights and one melt down at Chillis. And then my barf face.

11:45am

HENRY: Classic Chilis Barf Face

12:15pm

MICHAEL: So what I'm hearing is that if I avoid Chili's, the trip should be a success?

Can I get a reading on either Bennigan's or TGIFriday's?

1:03pm

HENRY: No trip is a failure that includes Chilis. I should've been more clear.

2:43pm

JAKE: Appleby's.

2:55pm

HENRY: All of these are American classics that should be honored.

3:12pm

FRENCH: Booze and a high chair.
And an 11 thousand calorie lunch.

5:22pm

PADRAIC: There is a baby flying bell curve. When they are really tiny, they just nurse and sleep. When they hit 3 or so, they are little people that you can reason with somewhat and distract with an iPad. But it's that middle period where they are proto-human squirmy balls of foul liquid that try to bring the entire plane down.

5:24pm

PADRAIC: When Freddy was a year old, I changed his diaper on a turbulent flight in a cramped bathroom with no changing table. Had to balance him on the toilet lid and make sure no important part of him touched any urine soaked surface. Then... I took a pee too. It was like cirque du soleil.

6:16pm

MICHAEL: 😫

6:16pm

MICHAEL: We're a day away from travel, and what have I had today? An assfull of this kid. An assfull, gentlemen.

6:49am

HENRY: I'm assuming mike is dead or he done run off. Happy Mother's Day mother fuckers. Proud of you all.

1:49pm

MICHAEL: ....we made it. It was...not great. But - we made it. I don't have to fly back do I?

6:04pm

HENRY: Lanahan you made it!!!

8:43pm

MICHAEL: *exhale*

8:43pm

MICHAEL: 😵‍💫

Seven Days Later...

8:46pm
VICTOR: How was the trip home?

8:47pm
MICHAEL: Flying with your kid for the first time feels a lot like deciding to have a second kid: You go on your first flight and there are good moments that punctuate the screams, and ugly looks from others. And you're thinking to yourself, "I'm in fucking hell right now!" and "I'm never doing this again!" And then you finally land, and the relief of it being over and the kind words of other passengers is such an enormous relief that shortly thereafter it's all you can remember. Then you think, "Well, sure it was a little tough, but we could do this again. Sure!"

8:48pm
MICHAEL: Admittedly, the trip out was total hell, but she was pretty great for the ride home, with exception of the last 30 minutes. Hmm...kinda makes me think i COULD do that again!

11:28pm
HENRY: Here we go. Lanahans are about to get knocked up again.

11:34pm
JAKE: Henry are you at Mike's house?

11:39pm
HENRY: They're both about to get knocked up. By me.

11:45pm
JAKE: 😎

173

POOPING IN THE TUB

8:46pm

VICTOR: Talk to me when your kids poop in the tub every other week. The last time I heard him grunt and I said "hey buddy no pooping in the tub." He looked up at me and smiled as carrot filled poop floated to the surface.

8:48pm

PADRAIC: When a three year old poops in the bath, it looks like a dolphin giving birth.

HENRY FLIES WITH THE BABY

7:08pm

HENRY: Okay. I can honestly say I've never needed a vacation so bad in my life. A whirlwind few weeks professionally, a 4 month old, family in town off and on all month. SO WHY DO WE HAVE TO FLY TO NEW YORK WITH A BABY TO GET TO THE AFOREMENTIONED VACATION!??? Sigh...... Fly?????????????

7:20pm

HENRY: Plane??????
Airport???????
(Cross country flight???????)

7:28pm

VICTOR: As long as you get to drop off the baby when you get there, it'll be all good.

7:46pm

HENRY: Ummmm. Nope. But we'll have lots of family dying to take shifts with her. And a mother in law who wants another grandchild so we can say we're gonna go fool around and sleep instead! Kidding not kidding.

1:47pm

PADRAIC: Someone in this group has to have another just so I don't feel like the stupid one.

PADRAIC: But don't stress, Dittles- flying with a 5 month old is much easier than a 1 year old. They are still small, so your legs won't go to sleep as they drape over you, they are still nursing so there's something to occupy them, and they don't get bored nearly as easily. We took Freddy on some crazy ass across the country trips when he was 10 weeks old, 5 months old, and 8 months old, and they were all pretty easy. It was the 18 month old trip that kicked our butt.

1:50pm

PADRAIC: I put Freddy in a drunken parade in 100 degree heat in New Jersey when he was 10 weeks old. GO TIGERS!

1:51pm

HENRY: She handled the flight pretty well! Getting her to sleep on the final leg was a challenge that led to 15-20 minutes of fussy crying, but Sarah put her in the Kataan and walked up and down the aisle til she slept and we were home free! Row to ourselves both flights helped a TON.

Then came the car ride. Hannah HATES the car. She screamed for an hour straight and was a fragile mess the rest of the night from the exhausted screaming and missed nap.

But she slept 8 hours last night and is still going. Matter

3:10am

of fact she just laughed in her sleep as I got up to pee. Love you guys like crazy. Really need you. Really appreciate you.

MICHAEL: Sorry to hear about the car. Hopefully that'll dissipate as the months go on. If not, you all can always travel by bike for the next 18 years. Have a GREAT trip!

9:09am

HENRY: You'd love that, dirty hippie.

11:41am

VICTOR: Dude!!! Non stop car crying is the worst! Sorry to hear that, but glad the plane trip was good. When are you back?

11:50am

HENRY: Back Wednesday. We're gonna try a different car seat and we are honestly grateful it's only in the car, so we know how to stop it!!!

11:52am

NINE DAYS LATER...

HENRY: We did it! She was such a champ. Slept last 2 1/2 hours of our flight to vegas from buffalo and into Burbank nearly lost it but we kept her distracted! PHEW!!! Southwest was a winner with our own row both flights east and west we bit the bullet and bought a third seat to guarantee success. Thanks for the guidance and support my brothers you assuaged my fears BIG TIME!!!!!

12:56pm

VICTOR: Congratulations!!!

1:01pm

1:33pm

HENRY:

2:36pm

JAKE:

3:11pm

MICHAEL: *phew*

3:24pm

HENRY: As I typed that update she was hanging on by a thread, taxiing!!! But we made it. And she didn't even melt down on the hour 45 drive to the airport!!!

6:53pm

JAKE: Hope you're settling in Hank... I'm sure it goes without saying, but I think I speak for everyone when I say that if anything had happened to you, Sarah would have been taken care of...

7:02pm

HENRY: She deserves to be moderately happy.

Hey you guys are smart. I like christopher moore, john Irving, jonathan tropper, tom Robbins. Anyone got a book to recommend? Starting to throw reading and exercise back into my life, any of you readings anything fun I can get on my nook???

10:02pm

JAKE: Reading AND exercise? Well, lah-dee-dah, Mr.-I-Have-Time-To-Be-A-Well-Rounded-Human-Being...

A Trip to the Stars by Nicholas Christopher would fit nicely into that oeuvre...

11:54pm

MICHAEL: I Could Punch You In The Face by Michael Lanahan seems academically appropriate right about now.

12:22am

JAKE: It really should be required reading...

4:14am

HENRY: To be Clear it's 4am and I'm awake. So don't be too impressed. I've yet to read or lift a single weight at this point. But I'll take the human contact mike!

A Fatigue of Babies

FRENCH: Hey, gents. Watch 16 and Pregnant on MTV. It'll make you feel like Nelson Mandela.

HENRY: At last. I shall!

FRENCH: But it'll also make you want to seize their babies.

HENRY: By modern #babylaw that's my right as a father.

JAKE: If the baby makes eye contact with you, then sure…

HENRY: Three seconds eye to eye and that's your baby.

11:53pm
PADRAIC: I have six babies in my garage that won't stop staring at me.

11:53pm
HENRY: That's the risk you take when you start claimin' babies.

11:55pm
PADRAIC: I can't even fit my car in there anymore.

7:39am
FRENCH: Baby hoarders.

7:57am
HENRY: So many babies.

8:03am
MICHAEL: Technically speaking, is that called a gaggle of babies? A herd? A murder?

8:03am
HENRY: A giggle? Gotta have it's own name. And this will be useful to us so let's get on this, Daddies!!! A giggle of babies.

8:22am
JAKE: Giggle: "The Duffys have a giggle of babies in their garage."

8:25am
HENRY: "That party was a mess, I got overrun by a whole giggle of babies"
Get in here paddy.

8:25am
PADRAIC: A vomit of babies? An exhaustion of babies?

9:03am
VICTOR: An exhaustion of babies seems about right.

9:55am
MICHAEL: A Fatigue of Babies?

9:56am

HENRY: Ooooooooooh!

10:16am

JAKE: 👍

10:36am

FRENCH: In China it's a dumpster of babies. But only in the feminine.

10:45am

PADRAIC: Only crazy people have more than one baby. Btw, why's my wife's tummy getting big?

TOOTH-BRUSHING

9:46am
HENRY: Hannah cut another tooth today. It's peeking out at me, a harbinger of sleepless nights perhaps. Explains some crappy nights of sleep this week!

11:03am
PADRAIC: You gotta start brushing it with that rubber thimble thing!

11:04am
HENRY: I have no idea what you're talking about. Really? And that's it right guys the rest of them just come in easy with no pain and no sleepless nights? Right? Fuck.

11:06am
PADRAIC: They have this rubber thing you can put on your finger so you can "brush" their teeth early on. No toothpaste- just the rubber thing.

11:29am
PADRAIC: I just do whatever Emily says. Maybe she was playing a practical joke on me.

11:38am

HENRY: I'm going to put that rubber thing on my finger. Then make one dozen really awesome sexual jokes to my wife. She will love it.

11:46am

PADRAIC: Then, if you really want to clean their teeth, you set it to vibrate and...wait. I know what that thing was....

SWEARING

4:43pm

JAKE: Not to deflect, but I thought you all would want to know: Blue said Fuck today…

5:26pm

HENRY: Fucking NICE! I'm sure this is news French can appreciate.

10:27pm

FRENCH: Why did Blue drop the bomb? I'm really curious.

10:30pm

JAKE: She's a crack mimic… Mom and Dad have to re-train themselves… She got a hold of Crystal's travel mug of steaming hot tea and started pouring it on the couch… I believe I dashed over with a "NonononoNONONO awww fucking hell!" … and Blue replied with her ador-able little sing-songy "fuuUUuuuck!"

10:37pm

FRENCH: That's nothing short of everything I thought It should be. Applause.

10:55pm

JAKE: ☺

9:14am

MICHAEL: Yes, we have yet to begin to curb our language here…yikes.

9:16am

VICTOR: Cindy has to tell me to watch my language all the time. Alex is going to be the kid with the potty mouth, because his dad can't control his language.

10:20am

HENRY: Fucking A.

BREAST FEEDING

8:18pm

FRENCH: The baby just took the bottle out of my hand, stood up and drank it like John Wayne. I don't like it.

8:18pm

HENRY: I wish my baby would take a bottle, period.

8:20pm

FRENCH: You always hope for the milestones, celebrate, then it's sort of terrifying.

8:21pm

HENRY: Babies all walk like John Wayne.

8:21pm

FRENCH: That's a fact. Are you doing okay?

8:36pm

HENRY: We're doing well. Honestly my only heartbreak is that Hannah won't take a bottle so I can't offer Sarah much relief in that way. But everything else is just love and gushing. I deal with some guilt when I'm away auditioning and working but Sarah is just lovely about it and we're grateful for the abundance.

8:36pm

HENRY: She'll take the bottle. She's stubborn but I... Well you know I'm equally so.

8:43pm

FRENCH: For the first two months Vanessa was a milk producing champion. The nurses at Cedars were stunned by the output. Then it just stopped. She's the Guns And Roses of breast feeding. 3 good albums and done. The baby didn't have much choice. Drink it or don't.

8:55pm

HENRY: We're lucky with the breast feeding. But the downside is Hannah doesn't want anything but boob. Can't blame her!! I also think she misses Sarah hard when she's away. Again, can't blame her.

8:59pm

HENRY: Hey guys when did you go from two feedings at night to one?

9:15pm

MICHAEL: It was at 9 months that we trained her to drop the 2am feed, so that we only had 8/8:30pm and then again between 4-5am. But we had to take a few (read: 5) days to train that out of her. I think you can do it earlier - there are certainly programs that say they can.

It just depends on what your needs are and how long you can maintain your situation. We probably should have done it sooner, but it was comfortable. But it got to a breaking point for Angela "the baby sucks on my boobs and I need some fucking sleep to live" Lanahan!

11:16am

FRENCH: Helene started sleeping through at about the same time. At 7 months she would do it once a week or so. We didn't really do anything. It just started happening.

11:24am

VICTOR: Alex started sleeping through the night at 6 months, as soon as we transferred him to his crib. Before that we had been co-sleeping so, he'd been feeding on demand during the night.

11:28pm

HENRY: Thanks fellas. Just gauging where we are at 6 months and where we "could/should" be.

CONSTIPATION

5:15pm

PADRAIC: Freddy hasn't pooped in three days. I asked him where his poop was, and he said his poop is eating lunch. Any ideas how to get him to poop?

5:17pm

HENRY: For real my baby hasn't in three days and we're freaking out. Is she sick or in trouble????

5:17pm

MICHAEL: baby laxative?

That's not unnormal Henry! At your baby's age once it's been 5-6 days without a poop, then call the doctor. 3 Yearold? I dunno...

5:19pm

PADRAIC: I wasn't kidding about Freddy- it's been three days. But I think if they're not exhibiting any bad signs, if they are eating and peeing and have energy, then just keep feeding them.

I think Freddy is fine- he's eating and playing and happy. But if we go another day or two, Im gonna text the doctor...

I probably should stop screaming "Poop!" At him.

5:25pm

MICHAEL: I dunno, it might scare the poop outta him.

5:26pm

PADRAIC: I yelled it so hard, I pooped myself.

5:27pm

JAKE: Will he eat apples? Or apple sauce?

5:33pm

PADRAIC: I just gave him carrots, strawberries, and apple juice.

5:36pm

JAKE: He's gonna geyser... I'm guessing around 2am...

5:43pm

PADRAIC: He's farting now. This is gonna get serious real soon.

5:45pm

JAKE: Do not fail to update us with any developments.

6:19pm

MICHAEL: I'd advise a two-layer diaper system, with a possible poop hammock hanging down between his knees as a 3rd layer of defense.

By the way, Poop Hammock will be playing Coachella next year.

8:00pm

PADRAIC: He just jumped out of the tub, declaring he had to poop. After ten seconds on the potty, he said, " I don't have to poop - maybe it's still eating lunch!" I'm very disturbed. In this narrative, we have to wait for his poop to finish lunch and then poop. We have to wait for his poop to poop.

10:45pm

JAKE: 👍

8:02am

PADRAIC: He did it. The poop pooped. Henry, what about your little lady?

8:13am

HENRY: Nada. But she doesn't seem uncomfortable. Giving her chamomile tea and today a warm bath. We hit day five I might worry but she's feeding and peeing so…?

8:33am

MICHAEL: Um…uh…I don't think she should be drinking Chamomile tea. That may have been a joke, though. I'm tired. So tired.

8:39am

HENRY: Pediatrician and lactation consultant recommended it for calming the stomach and moving the bowels. It's an ingredient in natural gripe waters. Why are you saying she shouldn't have it???

12:04pm

MICHAEL: Gripe water is the stuff of Life over here. I should have bought stock…

3:09pm

HENRY: Pooooooooooop! She pooped.
There's mustard gold in them thar hills!!!

3:50pm

PADRAIC: Aww, I remember when they pooped mustard. Those were the good old days. Now he shits human shit. That's not so good.

3:58pm

HENRY: Sarah sent me a picture, I will spare you all.

5:37pm

FRENCH: Helene has been constipated so it's been flaxseed-a-Palooza. When it kicks in she's starts shuffling her legs and moving her hips. Vanessa's assessment? "Check out Axl Rose."

5:54pm

VICTOR: nice

7:01pm

JAKE: That's exactly how I imagine Axl with explosive bowel-movements…

190

9:31pm

JAKE: Blue has taken to lying about poop... "Papa, I have poops!" is never true, merely a tactic to draw attention in the 5 seconds we're actually discussing something else. However, uncomfortable silence with grimacing, and then a sharp "No!" to our inquiry about whether she just pooped = guaranteed poop...

10:39pm

MICHAEL: Fuckin' poops. Goddamn, fuckin' poops.

10:58pm

VICTOR: We bought a potty for Alex just so he can get used to seeing it around. Lately he's started saying he has to pee, and goes and sits on his potty. Then asks for toilet paper, which he puts behind his back, before getting up and putting it in the toilet and flushing.

Clearly he's been watching Mommy pee more than Daddy.

7:26am

FRENCH: Thanks to the potty cam - we all have.

8:27am

HENRY: PottyCam™, a division of Daddy Drinks™

8:35am

PADRAIC: Freddy just recently did potty from start to finish on his own! Including wiping! My work is now done. Good thing I have the explosive fire extinguisher phase of pooping to look forward to with the next one.

8:42am

HENRY: Great job Freddy!!!!

FIRST WORDS

8:47pm

FRENCH: We got first words today. I said "Hi" and waved. She did the same. Then Vanessa waved and said "Hi." And she did it again. So... "Hi."

8:52pm

VICTOR: Awesome!!!

9:29pm

JAKE: HI!

9:31pm

HENRY: Hi!!!!!!!!!!
Lovely. Great day brother!

11:01pm

MICHAEL: Wonderful! Also: Hi!

11:50pm

PADRAIC: Yay words! So great.

DISNEYLAND

—————— 🥃 ——————

9:31am

HENRY: I heard there's a treasure hunt somewhere in the Magic Kingdom. Google "Magic Kingdom treasure hunt," you get clues and a map, which makes me think it may be in Adventureland or near New Orleans or the pirate stuff? I just read about it on Facebook "10 things you never knew about Disneyland" and it looked awesome. For kids!

9:33am

HENRY: Do not go on nemo's ride (formerly 20,000 leagues under the sea), it is a complete ripoff, and feels like you are about to drown in a tin can with 30 weird sweaty strangers. Do not go on that ride!

9:36am

HENRY: For future visits, multiple day multiple park, I recommend getting a room at the grand Californian Hotel! You get into the park early on certain days, and you can just go ride rides for a few hours then go lay by the pool take a nap etc. The worst thing about these parks is trying to do the whole park in 10 hours in extreme heat, a break multiple times throughout the day really helps!

9:37am

HENRY: Also maybe bring an umbrella? Might be a really great way to keep the sun off of you when you are standing in line. That is your old lady advice of the day.

11:00am

MICHAEL: I recommend Walt Disney's: Hall of Anti-Semites. It's a little off the beaten path, but fascinating. And the kids get a free button in the shape of a star when they leave!

12:09pm

PADRAIC: It's sponsored by Ford.

THE JOY OF POOPING ALONE

6:01pm

VICTOR: I'm pooping.

6:02pm

PADRAIC: Good work.

It's just you and me. I'm here to help you through this.

How's it going?

Are you alone, or is a baby staring at you?

6:06pm

VICTOR: It's good. There's nothing better than the after work poop.

Mommy has the baby, so daddy has quiet time.

I stay until my legs fall asleep or Alex starts banging on the door.

6:08pm

PADRAIC: I don't leave until I've used up all of my lives on candy crush

6:09pm

VICTOR: Ha! My current choice is 2048. But I may need something new as I beat that this morning.

Have you played 2048…?

6:10pm

PADRAIC: You mean the game where I pretend it's the year I get to resume my writing career?

6:11pm

VICTOR: ...yes... It's wonderful and depressing at the same time.

6:14pm

PADRAIC: A slogan for parenting if I've ever heard one.

6:19pm

MICHAEL: 👍

6:20pm

VICTOR: It's amazing how quickly my legs fall asleep nowadays. Gotta go!

6:22pm

MICHAEL: Well, then you get to play the sorry-honey-my-legs-don't-work-you-have-to-watch-the-baby-some-more ploy.

Works eeeeevery time.

6:24pm

PADRAIC: Then you can play the "I can't feel my penis" game.

6:33pm

VICTOR: You mean I'm supposed to be able to feel my penis?

6:33pm

PADRAIC: No one else is gonna.

6:36pm

VICTOR: Ain't that the truth!

7:16pm

JAKE: 👍

11:40pm

PADRAIC: Late night dumps are a beautiful thing.

11:43pm

VICTOR: Indeed. The others are sleeping. The house is still. It's so quiet I hate to break it up with my pooping, but then it feels so good. The pooping that is.

1:41am

JAKE: Sometimes when I take a monster dump in the middle of a hot day I end up completely naked by the end.

7:14am

HENRY: I'm reading this on a naked morning dump while Hannah gets her diaper changed.

Also my wife now says di-ah-per. I won that battle.

8:08am

MICHAEL: I knew I had finally won when I could leave my daughter unattended to go take a dump. Great day.

4:27pm

PADRAIC: When I poop, Freddy raids the kitchen cabinets for candy. Casually. He casually raids the kitchen cabinets for candy. I take a long time to poop.

4:35pm

FRENCH: I poop at eleven. Like a Swiss clock. If I don't, I write rude emails.

4:39pm

HENRY: I enjoy those non-poop emails. They're charming.

FEVERS

FRENCH: Helene has had a fever. So I'm watching some really fucked up, hippy shit on The Baby First Channel.

HENRY: I'm scared to watch that channel. I assume it's babies with underarm hair. My baby shaves her pits.

PADRAIC: Fevers suck. They burn so hot and get so sad. Freddy got over 104 last week and it still scares the crap out of me. I put a wet hand towel in the freezer for ten minutes, then put it on his head. I wanted to put Freddy in the freezer, but the book we had said that would "kill" him.

HENRY: "Book"

JAKE: Books are helpful.

HENRY: Here we go, freaking liberal intellectualism.

8:32am

JAKE: Crystal does the book-larnin in our family... we went ER at 102 a few months ago... terrifying…

8:38am

PADRAIC: We try to not give any medication unless it's over 103. And we try to not bother our doctor unless we get over 105. (The big caveat is if they are showing other symptoms, all bets are off. You know when it's just a fever - then you can wait until it gets really bad and hit it with some ibuprofen. But if they have a rash, or a raspy cough, or vomit - get them help.)

8:38am

PADRAIC: If they get over 110, then do their bidding, for they are the dark lord.

8:41am

JAKE: Not awesome? Holding down a screaming baby for an x-ray and/or IV while they implore you with "Why are you allowing this to happen?" in their eyes…

8:55pm

VICTOR: Ok, highest fever you child has had? Alex set a personal best at 103.5 yesterday (Non-stop hits!) and his fever continues today. Not gonna lie, that freaks me out a bit.

9:12pm

PADRAIC: Freddy's record is 104.5. And high fevers are the scariest thing I've been through. You feel completely helpless. Usually Freddy's fevers will start to go away in the morning and we think we're through the woods. And then late afternoon it roars back.

9:14pm

MICHAEL: I can't come close to anything more than 101.something.

9:24pm

VICTOR: Paddy, that's exactly what happened to Alex. I'm sure he's fine, but it still sucks.

FATHER'S DAY

8:00am
HENRY: Happy Father's Day, mother f-ers!!!!!
I cherish you men. On and off this thread. Pure love. Enjoy getting celebrated today.

9:34am
MICHAEL: Happy Father's Day each and every one of you. You deserve it for helping raise such beautiful, amazing children!

9:49am
PADRAIC: The most important day of the year in the daddy drinks calendar! Happy dad day, gentlemen. You are all awesome dads!

HENRY: Steak and blowjob day!!!

Right???

Aw crap

Best part of my gift (She knows me):

11:03am

MICHAEL:

10:27am

11:50am

VICTOR: Happy Father's Day, Gentlemen! It's an honor to know you.

12:08pm

MICHAEL: Side note: I think it's weird that you let your daughter go to a liquor store on her own to buy you booze for Father's Day.

12:09pm

HENRY: Do you think it's weird, mike? DO you?

12:09pm

VICTOR: Don't be a prude, Lanahan!

12:39pm

MICHAEL: *sigh* I'm just jealous.

1:41pm

PADRAIC; If only it were steak and blowjob day.

The last time my penis was near a face was when Freddy walked over, pointed at my junk and laughed.

2:19pm

HENRY: He tweeted right after. It was hilarious. Sorry.

2:20pm

PADRAIC: Damn that kid! Btw, all you need to do is add Nazis to the list, and you have my wife's three least favorite things in the world, in this order:
1)blowjobs
2)Steak
3) Nazis

2:40pm

MICHAEL: In that order, by the way.

3:43pm

JAKE: Imma catch up on your Nazi-Steak-Blowjob convo later, but happiness upon all of you…

11:26pm

FRENCH: Happy Fathers Day. I love you guys. Truly.

11:27pm

MICHAEL: It's Father's Day, so I just want to say this: A while back, I said to a few of you what a difficult time I was having with Fatherhood. It'd been nearly nine+ months of misery, frustration, and exhaustion - and I spent a good deal of time wondering whether I'd made a huge mistake. I can't put my finger on it, but in the last 2 to 3 months, Finley has really changed, and developed (and so have I), and what started as a hint of light in the distance at the end of the tunnel has really grown into a blinding light, and I just love being around her, and I'm really loving being a father and this journey. God, I can't get enough of her - even when she's miserable like today during my 2nd Father's Day. ☺

I just wanted to thank you guys, not only for listening to me that night, but also for being there when I needed you. Having a baby is fucking crazy. #babylaw

11:29pm

PADRAIC: I'm just sitting by myself, buzzed on some fancy beer, looking at endless pictures of my friends and their fathers, or my friends with their children, and thinking about how exhausted and happy my son makes me, and I just gotta say I love being a dad, and I love that I get to share what it feels like with you fine gentlemen.

11:37pm

FRENCH: Helene had been sick for a week. Turned the corner on Fathers Day. I didn't get to see her. Two shows. I have a banged up hip and weird looking elbow. Was actually happy when she woke up tonight. Happy Fathers Day, Gents.

11:39pm

FRENCH:

11:40pm

PADRAIC: You gotta put a steak on that. Or get a blowjob.

Or Nazi. Something about a nazi.

11:44pm

FRENCH: You are my new least favorite Duffy.

11:45pm

PADRAIC: You sound like my wife.

11:52pm

FRENCH: Yeah I do. I'm hot, talented and don't want to bed you .

11:54pm

PADRAIC: But still, I sneaked a baby in her! Which means, I sneaked a baby in you.

12:07pm

FRENCH: Crap

I think we can agree you'll never sneak anything into Emily again. Baby or otherwise.

2:02am
FRENCH: Happy Father's Day, gents. I love you.

10:36am
JAKE: I'm laughing out loud through my tequila hang-over (#sheknowsme), alone at my computer... Thanks to you all: this group makes me feel a part of something in a way I haven't for a long-ass time...

11:59am
HENRY: Like like like like like.

1:32pm
MICHAEL: Ditto

KIDS' CLASSES

PADRAIC: Sitting in the bleachers at swim class. Yes, I'm that parent now.

Have you guys put your kids in classes yet?

MICHAEL: Currently she's teaching a class on kicking my ass, but that's it.

HENRY: Sarah takes her to mommy and me yoga. Not the same thing. I can't wait to make Hannah learn to do all the things I never wanted to do.

VICTOR: Alex has started swimming classes with Cindy. I'd go, but I don't like to get wet.

HENRY: Too easy. Must resist softball "wet" setup... Must... Resist...

10:07pm

PADRAIC: Your wife likes to get wet! The last time I made my wife wet was when I put too much in the washer and the kitchen flooded. Every noun just then was a euphemism.

3:55am

HENRY: Even "wife?"

12:10pm

PADRAIC: Emily keeps signing Freddy up for shit, and then at the last second, she can't do it and I have to. So in an hour, I have to take Freddy to a nature walk with a Ranger or something. I just want to sit at home and drink coffee and poop.

12:14pm

FRENCH: You're gonna get a handy from a ranger in a Griffith Park bathroom.

BABY SHOES

FRENCH: How do you know what size shoe to get for a baby.

VICTOR: You have to take them to a baby shoe store and get them fitted

FRENCH: Thanks. She's walking a lot and wants to go outside.

VICTOR: yeah, you gotta protect them feetsies just get the soft bottom shoes. They'll allow her to feel the ground more

PADRAIC: Baby shoes are really fun to buy.

Enjoy the fact that you get to choose. Once she gets older, she will have an opinion, and then you end up with green plastic shoes with tassels and chewbaca's face on it that lights up and roars with each step.

11:49am

HENRY: And where would one find those shoes in adult sizes?

12:01pm

VICTOR: The Pleasure Chest on Santa Monica

12:06pm

JAKE: We have enough shoes to last until she's 5... they just keep appearing...

12:23pm

HENRY: Hannah's grown out of more shoes than she'll ever wear.

Moms love to buy them. Babies don't need them.

12:33pm

PADRAIC: If they can't walk, they don't need shoes. We did learn that letting Freddy decide which shoes he wants to wear when we go out was a great way to let him feel empowered. But then he wants to wear hiking boots to swim class, and it all goes to shit.

TAKING FIRST SHIFT

FRENCH: 💔
6:37am

HENRY: French, why the heartbreak???
7:00am

FRENCH: Because it's Saturday morning and I've been awake since 5:50. 💔
7:33am

HENRY: Boooo! This was me two nights ago. Baby slept perfectly. I was up at 3am and never got back down. Last night I could've slept perfectly but she fidgeted all night. Feel for you brother, I can only imagine jet lag ain't helpin'.
8:03am

MICHAEL: I think it's convenient that when Angela is on morning duty, she rolls out of bed at 7:30, but when I'm on duty, I'm up from 5:30 on. I just think she ignores her daughters cries better than I do.
9:51am

10:29am

HENRY: Bottom line we are better parents than our wives are?

12:36pm

JAKE: Baby law.
Crystal can sleep through a freakin earthquake

12:06am

PADRAIC: I have pretended to be asleep so that my pregnant wife will get up with Freddy. Ashamed? Yes. A little more rested? Double yes.

1:22am

JAKE: 👍

You Can Have My BOB When You Pry It From My Cold, Dead Fingers

---

12:49pm

JAKE: Could anyone (ahem, PADRAIC!) use a Graco 35 rear-facing car seat with base? Yours free... I'll even clean it up for you... I'll throw in the BOB stroller attachment too...

1:14pm

FRENCH: I would also chip in some previously sharted garments. Free.

2:09pm

HENRY: There's our guy! Please tell me the sharted items in question are adult size for male, not baby size for girl. Do any of you have a BOB stroller you don't use? Or any kind of running stroller? I really would love to have one for Hannah and would use it every day probably.

2:29pm

JAKE: You can have my BOB when you pry it from my cold, dead fingers.

2:31pm

VICTOR: I'm with Jake. And I haven't even used mine to run yet.

Buy one, it's expensive, but so worth it

2:32pm

HENRY: How about I borrow yours for sayyyyyy 3 years?

2:34pm

FRENCH: If I get a tumor that clouds my judgement, you can have mine.

2:36pm

HENRY: Wait you all have a BOB???? dang!!!!!

2:53pm

VICTOR: BOBs are the shit. Even just for everyday use.

3:03pm

FRENCH: It's like a Hummer with a baby in it.

3:05pm

VICTOR: For a second, I was like "WHAT?!!?" And then I realized you meant the automobile….

3:10pm

VICTOR: 😱

3:33pm

MICHAEL: *sigh* Ive got a City Mini, and Angela has run with it. It's cheaper than a BOB.

5:19pm

HENRY: You all have running strollers. Dammit.

WHEN THE FAMILY'S AWAY...

7:15am

JAKE: I'm in Week 2 of bachelor life... Jake is a dull boy...

7:57am

MICHAEL: Are you in a baby-less bachelor life?? Tell us all about it! Spare no detail! Is it quiet? How's the sleep? And YES let's get together!

8:49am

JAKE: I sleep like a rock. 5-6hrs at night + 1 in the afternoon.

9:01am

MICHAEL: 😎

9:10am

JAKE: When I pick things up off the floor, they remain off the floor.
No one wears the dog food bowl as a hat.

9:23am

VICTOR: Umh! Don't stop now...
Can you take a dump in peace?

9:27am
FRENCH: Is there food on the floor?

9:28am
HENRY: Tell us jake we wanna know!

9:36am
MICHAEL: Do your personal items end up in the trash bin?

10:01am
JAKE: No one waits until they have clean clothes and a fresh diaper to drop a load.

I haven't had to search for a remote once.

10:23am
MICHAEL: Yeah, but you can't just come and go as you please, right?

10:24am
JAKE: No one finds their dark blue washable crayon particularly delicious, gnawing on it until it seeps and bubbles out around her face in a partial Jolson...

Yesterday I was going to go out, but decided not to autonomously...

10:29am
VICTOR: What?!?!? That's crazy!!!
What did you do??

10:31am
JAKE: I worked peacefully at the computer, uninterrupted.

Then I took a nap.

10:31am
VICTOR: A nap....?
Do those things still exist?

10:31am
JAKE: ... in the living room...

10:31am
VICTOR: AH!!!!

10:31am
JAKE: ... which was quiet...

10:32am
VICTOR: ...I ...I just....I can't even imagine.

10:33am

PADRAIC: Can you make love to your own body without hiding in the guest room closet?

I may have shared too much.

10:38am

JAKE: What do you think those living room naps are all about?

10:40am

MICHAEL: Padraic is asking the questions we really want the answers to.

11:12am

FRENCH: I just cleaned an explosion, of The Artist Formerly Known As Yogurt, from a diaper.

How long has Sidney been on furlough?

11:23am

PADRAIC: How long before he realizes they just left him for some guy named Rick?

11:41am

FRENCH: Crystal is trying to convince Blue that it's okay to hug Rick. Rick can't be trusted to refill The Wheel of Fortune machine with nickels at the Golden Nugget. But she loves him.

11:42am

PADRAIC: But he's your new daddy. Isn't it nice to have a new daddy?

11:50am

FRENCH: And he looks almost exactly like Jake. Almost.

11:55am

PADRAIC: Things will be different now, she thinks. Things will be different.

4:21pm

JAKE: I hope Rick likes doing dishes…

4:39pm

VICTOR: Rick is a dick. I only put up with him for Blue's sake.

5:34pm

JAKE: 👍

9:11pm

MICHAEL: Gentlemen, we just dropped our daughter off at her Grandparents tonight. And we don't pick her up until late Monday afternoon. I'm...excited. I'm ecstatic. I'm going to sleep so much. I told Angela I'm closing the blinds and walking around naked with an erection all weekend. Why? Because I can.

That's why.

10:06pm

JAKE: Surely she'll help you out with that situation…

10:54pm

VICTOR: Why close the blinds?

MOMMY PHASE

7:04pm

HENRY: Well we have had some really great developments, including longer naps and Hannah starting the night in her crib until about 11 PM for her first feeding. But there has been a really SHITTY development where she will not let me rock her to sleep. The second I try to rock her to sleep she loses her mind. Sarah shot a commercial this week and I'm just wondering if it's because Sarah was away for a whole day and she got some separation anxiety, because it never really happened before then. Anyone else experience this along the way? It sucks.

7:40pm

MICHAEL: Hank, that's just development. She's changing, and the shit that worked yesterday, ain't working now and you've got to improvise til you find something that works. It could very well be Sarah's absence, but the point remains: you gotta dance, Monkey! (or in your case: stop dancing.)

8:05pm

HENRY:

8:22pm

PADRAIC: Freddy went through a long period when he wouldn't let me do anything (I don't want daddy to read me a story!) and he more than once has said "I DON'T love daddy." So I think they go through these developmental stages where they drift to and away from their Daddy. But you gotta know that no matter what they say, they love you just as much.

8:39pm

HENRY: No matter what you guys say? I love all of YOU just as much.

10:16pm

MICHAEL: Finley is 70% Mommy all the time, and then goes thru a hard-core BRIEF Daddy-lovin' phase. Then that turns off. And the whole time Angela is, like, "My daughter doesn't love me anymore!". There's a lot of ebb and flow. And for us: shuck and jivin'!

10:35pm

VICTOR: When Alex wakes up in the morning he wimpers softly to let us know he's awake. Nothing serious. He even stops when we're walking down the hall so he can hear if we're coming into his room or the bathroom. If Cindy goes in, he gets happy and screams "Mommy!" If I go in he starts hardcore crying and screaming "Mommy!" #sometimesmykidisajerk

10:53pm

MICHAEL: OH MY GOD! I'm the same Victor. The moment Finley sees me walk in the door she screams and flails! Apparently she's forgotten the first six months when I came in to get her first, and only remembers the last few when Angela mostly went in first.

10:54pm

PADRAIC: I think they are programmed to push us away because we could eat them.

10:55pm

MICHAEL: WILL eat them

218

10:56pm
PADRAIC: It's not uncommon for Freddy to respond to my friendly "good morning" with a "no!" And then he pushes me away.

At what age are you not allowed to eat your kid?

10:59pm
MICHAEL: I don't know that there is a statute of limitations. I'm not really familiar with law. I'm an actor. I say things with feeling.

7:02am
FRENCH: I haven't seen that, Mike.

God. It used to be that if we were up at 7 it was because we had a nose fulla blow.

8:15am
HENRY: Or were sitting in the ocean, surfing, waiting for waves.

8:18am
PADRAIC: Or eating other peoples children.

8:18am
HENRY: Yes of course. Or eating other peoples children.

LAST night hannah wouldn't sleep and Sarah couldn't get her down because the rocker was squeaking. Cut to Hank, naked at midnight with tools and lubricant in his hands breaking a sweat. THAT used to have a whole new meaning too. Didn't it? Can't remember.

9:14am
JAKE: Can we have cocaine at the next Daddy Drinks event?

9:38am
HENRY: 👍

9:54am
PADRAIC: Can we take a nap first?

9:56am
HENRY: Oooooooh!!!

10:07am
PADRAIC: So Freddy's ready for his sister. I asked him what the first thing he's gonna say to her is, and he replied "don't make everything dirty."

11:02am

HENRY: He's fucking right paddy. Jeez.

11:34am

JAKE: 👍

11:53am

HENRY: It's tough. I do everything around the house to make up for Sarah constantly needing to feed and soothe the baby. I'm not deadbeating it, man. So Sarah goes to get her hair done or take a break and all my girl does is scream. I can soothe her at night. I can change her. But this daytime shit is pretty defeating. This is my one stumbling block so far. And it's beating me the fuck up for sure.

11:54am

HENRY: Sarah has to be able to leave. And I need to be able to watch Hannah during the day. But so far it's just me grabbing five minutes of calm here and there and treading water til Sarah gets home. At which point she feels guilty like she can never leave which is no good either.

Bottom line, no matter how fucked up things get the next two hours? When Sarah comes home I'm going have to tell her everything was perfect. Shit.

11:55am

HENRY: One brief exception, is that I hold her in my arms facing away from me and keep her in motion. The question is how long can I keep this up? Dear God how long?! Ha!!!!!

12:05pm

VICTOR: Yeah. I remember that. It got easier later, but he would be awesome while she was there and then scream bloody murder when she was gone. If she'd call to check in I wouldn't answer cuz I didn't want her to know how horrible it was going. I felt so useless. The good news is, it gets better. Just hang in there and get breaks when you can. I'm at Barney's watching games all day if you can catch a break.

12:11pm

HENRY: I can't catch a break because the only time I can leave is to run to auditions or jobs and get back home. But thank you for this Victor I really needed it. I put her in a swaddle which I'm trying not to do in the daytime but it is working. I'm walking around with the football hold, which I didn't think I'd have to do in the daytime, but any means necessary right now. Really thanks brother I needed it.

12:14pm

VICTOR: Dude, the first three months is Malcolm X time: By any means necessary! Swaddle her, football hold her, dress up like Liza Minelli and sing puff the magic dragon to her. Whatever it takes. Just survive.

12:19pm

HENRY: Holy shit, it worked. I soothed her to sleep and slipped her in her swing with the sleep sheep for good measure. I'd already jogged a few miles with the stroller before the meltdown so now lifting weights for as long as this sanity lasts! I will not be defeated. THANKS VIC

3:01pm

VICTOR: I'm day drunk!

INAPPROPRIATE BABY USAGE VI: BUTT THAT BABY!

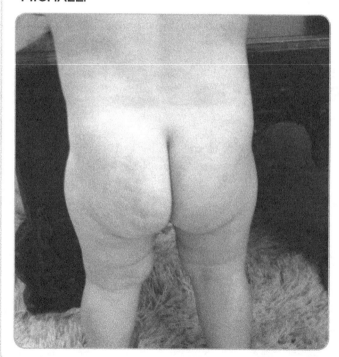

MICHAEL: Bonus points if your child pees on your $300 rug while you're trying to capture that tush!

(Freddy is exempt because he's not a baby. But when that new baby gets here...)

8:49am

HENRY: 👍

11:34am

JAKE:

11:56am

HENRY: Buns!!!!!!!!!

11:59am

HENRY:

2:03pm

HENRY: Did I do this right?

2:03pm

4:19pm

JAKE: It's working for me...

I don't think we should give Padraic a pass...

"Emily, you good with the baby? Cool... I'll be taking some pictures of Freddy in the bathroom..."

"Mommy?"

4:21pm

VICTOR: I'm conflicted about Dittman's picture...

5:12pm

PADRAIC: Henry, you did that right. You did that very right.

5:14pm

MICHAEL: I would like to make Henry today's "Daddy Drinks Hero!" And apparently #ButtThatWife will become a thing now.

9:24pm

VICTOR: I'm still too conflicted about Ditty's picture to comment.

10:07pm

MICHAEL: Clock's ticking to Butt That Baby everyone (including Henry!).

6:26am

HENRY: I'm looking forward to another day of mike asking us to take pics of our children's butts and us not responding. It's gonna get awkward for him soon.

7:58am

MICHAEL: Butts, guys. Amirght?!

9:02am

JAKE: 👍

11:30am

HENRY: Sigh. Yes, Michael. I suppose.

12:18pm

PADRAIC: The more we talk, the more scrolling up I have to do to see Dittman's picture.

BABYSITTERS

PADRAIC: Let's talk about babysitters.

HENRY: What the hell is a babysitter?

PADRAIC: A person you pay to watch your TV.

HENRY: And do they make more per hour than most people we know???

PADRAIC: If only Emily would pay me to watch my kids - we'd be rich!

HENRY: French is on a network show, he should pay us all to watch our kids. I voted for Obama, where's all that juicy socialism I was promised?!?! (Warned about, tomato tomahto)

1:24pm

FRENCH: Stop it

1:24pm

HENRY: Just pay me, French. No one else is here. They'll never know.

Just me. C'mon.

1:25pm

FRENCH: No

1:25pm

HENRY: C'moooooooon.

1:26pm

FRENCH: No

1:27pm

HENRY: Thanks a lot, Obama!

4:38pm

PADRAIC: Lets all just pay each other. Like a parenting circle jerk.

4:47pm

PADRAIC: And silence.

7:28pm

VICTOR: Uh…is Henry's wife in the circle? Cuz I might consider that.

Too soon?

7:42pm

HENRY: Oh Victor. Soon you'll never have sex again. Ever. Never ever.

And yes, she is.

7:48pm

VICTOR: Soon?

7:58pm

PADRAIC: I've heard of this thing called sex. It's what unicorns do all day in Neverland! (He says sarcastically, already forgetting that sex is a real thing he used to do with that lady he now just stares at at 3 in the morning tiredly in between diaper changes)

8:37pm

HENRY: Dude don't stare too long she's super fertile and you have zero will power.

9:38pm

HENRY: Hey guys what are you paying babysitters? Curious about night time going out rates versus daytime an hour here and there while we run to auditions rates. I know $20 is a going rate but that seems outrageous is that always what you pay? Also why did we go to college we should've just been babysitters $20 an hour is fucking amazing.

9:40pm

VICTOR: We actually pay our mainstay babysitter $15 an hour. And she is AMAZING with Alex. Came to us on a recommendation from Dean and Jessie. If I remember she may have differing rates, but we just pay her $15 (the higher rate) all the time.

I can't remember what the lower rate is or when it's applicable

Also, I'd totally introduce you to her. She's amazing!

10:07pm

HENRY: We would love that but I would hate to poach your babysitter.

10:08pm

VICTOR: we're not the only one she works for and it can be quite distressing finding someone to leave your heart with, so....

If you want, I'll ask if I can pass along her info to you

hmmm, is this a time I should ask my wife about it first?

10:35pm

HENRY: YES.

YES YOU ASK YOUR WIFE FIRST BEFORE GIVING OUT YOUR NUMBER ONE BABYSITTER'S PHONE NUMBER. ALSO WE HAVE OPTIONS, I WILL ASK YOU IF WE FEEL LIKE WE NEED HER, AND I REALLY APPRECIATE YOU OFFERING.

That was not supposed to be in all capital letters but I don't have the energy to go back and change it.

11:00pm

JAKE: It's a little shouty in here…

11:02pm

FRENCH: It's because Ditty is screaming at Victor.

227

11:03pm

VICTOR: ...why is he screaming at me? I was only trying to help....

11:05pm

FRENCH: It made him mad when you respected your wife's opinion.

11:20pm

HENRY: NO IT MADE ME MAD WHEN HE DID NOT RESPECT HIS WIFE'S OPINION. wait. What happened? I'm dizzy. I told him to ask her and...

I'm out of the group again aren't I?

12:08am

PADRAIC: and our baby-sitter is great and charges $17 an hour. Although Emily is always rounding up. That's gonna be the death of me. The rounding up.

1:03am

MICHAEL: Oh the fucking rounding up....

1:06am

MICHAEL: Our #1 Nanny goes for $12/hr, which is the going rate down here. Plus we have a neighbor as our back-up and since she just walks four feet to get here she only charges $10/hr, but that's a steal and we use her every chance we can. We got our #1 nanny on Care. com. Totally vetted and certified nannies/babysitters on the site, and she was the 3rd or 4th we interviewed. It's a really good option, after word-of-mouth.

1:09am

VICTOR: What the hell does she round up to??? 17.50?!?

1:16am

HENRY: Thanks for the advice guys I appreciate it more than you know.

And I feel the love. ☺

2:04am

MICHAEL: Without local family, you HAVE to find a regular sitter, and a back-up. Ours are becoming increasingly unavailable, and we're starting to get nervous, and not looking forward to starting the hunt over again.

2:50am

HENRY: This is why I resisted taking Vic's sitter's number. It happens. And seems to be looming most of the time unless you lock them down full time.

2:55am

FRENCH: I'm thrilled to say that our nanny bench is three deep. Robert Horry, James Worthy and someone else who's a solid nanny.

FIRST
HAIRCUT

12:41pm
VICTOR:

12:56pm
HENRY: Handsome gentleman!!!!

1:05pm

JAKE: playa…

6:48pm

MICHAEL: Soooooth Operator!

7:49am

HENRY: What the hell is a sooth operator, mike? That some Shakespeare shit I don't know about?

2:05pm

MICHAEL: "m"s are hard.

I RUNNING RUNNING!

3:12pm

VICTOR: Alex's new game is "NO. Stop it! I running running!"

3:19pm

VICTOR: For instance, in the morning when we leave for daycare, we walk out the door and I open the car door and say "Let's go, buddy." And most days, he replies with "My turn," meaning he wants to climb into his car seat on his own. Some days, he puts his hands up and says "Grab it." At least that's what I think he says, we're not really sure and multiple attempts to figure out what he's saying or where it came from have failed.

3:20pm

VICTOR: And then there are the days where he says "No." He tries to close the car door, but I don't let him and he says "Stop it!"

"Come on, buddy, get in the car."

"No!"

Then he slowly backs down the driveway, never taking his eyes off me. Measuring the distance so he knows when I won't be able to close the distance too quickly.

"Alex, come get in the car."

"No, stop it!"

And as soon as he gets to the sidewalk, he turns and takes off, "I running running!"

And, of course, I have to take off after him, which sends him into a stampeding, giggle fit.

Needless to say, Daddy is tired of this game, so I came up with a counter measure.

He is currently going through a little separation anxiety, so leaving him causes him to run after you. And I'm not above using a toddler's neurosis against him.

So, he starts backing down the driveway, with a wry little smile on his face, knowing I'm going to chase him, but I didn't even ask him to get into the car a second time. I just closed the door and started to walk around to the driver's side of the car.

"OK, buddy, I'm gonna-"

Now we've had the not going into the street talk for a while now. And he doesn't. He'll grab one of our hands before he enters the street on most occasions. And besides, when we play this game, he gets to the sidewalk and runs down the sidewalk....normally.

"OK, buddy, I'm gonna-" He turned and ran straight for the street, laughing up a storm. I thought "He better slow down or he's not gonna make the turn. HOLY SHIT HE'S RUNNING TO THE STREET!!!!"

I high tailed it and grabbed him right as his first foot hit the street. I spun him around and said "Hey! No running into the street!"

To which he replied, "Hahahaha! Daddy!"

How old do they have to be before we can shake the shit out of them again?

Alex 75 - Daddy 1

MICHAEL: You better tan that hide!!
5:01pm

JAKE: It's pretty funny, though, you gotta admit... Not to Victor, but to everyone else...
5:43pm

First Steps for Finley

12:57pm

MICHAEL: Finley's walking! It's pretty amazing, and wonderful and scary.

6:08pm

HENRY: Mike!!! Walking??? Yeah Finley!! Now if you'll excuse me I have to carry my lazy-ass baby all over the damn place.

9:27pm

VICTOR: My kids been walking for months and his lazy ass still doesn't have a job. I told him this morning that he'd better get on getting a job or get on getting a new place to stay. I ain't raising no bums!

10:34pm

MICHAEL: Forget all the nice new toys she got for her birthday, these tiny feet just wanna walk the walk!

12:28am

FRENCH: Fantastic.

12:42am

HENRY: Love it!!!!!!
Does she love walking??

12:57am

MICHAEL: It's all she wants to do.

10:06am

FRENCH: I wasted so much time being angry the other day. Then Helene took a quantum leap. Walking with a push car. Just sort of strolling herself on it. It erased everything else. Really fun. Weepy as hell.

12:02pm

JAKE: Yesterday Blue made up a song about pants. It went, roughly: "Paants, paants, PAAANts... Paants, Paants, PAAAAAAAAAANNNTS!!!!"

They really do help put bullshit in its place.

12:58pm

FRENCH: Pants indeed.

INAPPROPRIATE BABY USAGE VII: BOWL & SPOON

11:18am
FRENCH: A bowl and a spoon. 7 bucks well spent.

11:19am
FRENCH:

HENRY: Oh my God she is gorgeous! What a big girl!

12:41pm

FRENCH: Thank you. Apparently no sleep gets you 4 teeth.

12:43pm

JAKE: Beautiful.

12:56pm

MICHAEL: I don't know...I might take the sleep over the teeth. But that could just be the sleeplessness talking, or my current disinterest in chewing.

12:59pm

HENRY: Chewing is for suckers mike. You're on the right track.

2:25pm

JAKE: We're not fancy with spoons and such…

7:24pm

VICTOR: 👍

8:17pm

FRENCH: 👍

8:21pm

HENRY: 👍

8:23pm

MICHAEL: I think I ordered that from a food truck once…

9:57pm

FRENCH: I love Blue. She's sittin' in a bowl like miso. Sweet face.

10:40pm

HENRY: Bowl challenge:

7:30am

Sarah: what are you doing?
Me: nothing babe.
Sarah: is this for your dad group???

Me: nope.

Sarah: want me to take the picture?

Me: no I have to do this for myself!!!

FRENCH: I once showed Vanessa a thread from Daddy Drinks and she proclaimed it "an atrocity to all that's right andnormal." Which I read as a win.

HENRY: Glorious.

TWO WEEKS UNTIL BABY CLARA

8:33am

MICHAEL: Guys: Paddy is, like, 2.5 weeks away. I'm starting to panic.

Can you all help me through this transition he's going through?

Some nights I dream that I'm Padraic, and I wake up screaming in a cold sweat.

9:17am

PADRAIC: Wait- I'm having what in 2 weeks? Does this have anything to do with my wife's beer belly?

9:20am

MICHAEL: Please, Padraic, this isn't about you.

9:53am

JAKE: Emily drinks beer now? Nice…

1:40pm

HENRY: Hey you guys, remember that guy padraic duffy? He was great.

2:29pm

FRENCH: He delivered a perfect son. And a lovely daughter is on the way. My question? Does Emily put him in the recycling bin or the biodegradable green container for leaves, poop, mulch and men who completed their biological mission and now have to go live in the Oakwood Apt's for discarded men?

3:03pm

JAKE: If you sprinkle some lye on him he'll break down naturally…

3:13pm

FRENCH: I'd prefer that to him breaking down at the Oakwood.apts.

3:35pm

HENRY: Everyone breaks down at the Oakwood. Why not use him in the Stewart Garden as compost?

3:38pm

FRENCH: He has two clear choices.
1-Live at the Oakwood.
2- Jake gradually breaks him down with lye.
I don't want Padraic haunting my garden.

3:56pm

PADRAIC: Your haunted garden will be filled with Boo-gonias. #ghostpuns

3:58pm

FRENCH: Crap. Will they benefit from Zom-Bee's?

4:20pm

MICHAEL: RIP Daddy Drinks thread.

4:22pm

PADRAIC: Here's the real question: if I live tweet the birth in Daddy Drinks, will my wife leave me?

4:52pm

VICTOR: I thought you were setting up a live stream with a couple of go pros, including one stuck to the baby's head so we can see what it's like passing through the birth canal?

10:50pm

MICHAEL: I feel like it's our responsibility as Daddy Drinks members to chip in and save Padraic by either 1) Killing him, or 2) providing him a whole new identity and life elsewhere in the country. I really only see those two options.

10:52pm

PADRAIC: My soft poet bones make terrible mulch.

FIRST STEPS
FOR HELENE

7:54am
FRENCH: Someone just took a few steps. I'm pretty excited.

8:22am
PADRAIC: If it was your baby- Yay! Congrats! If it was you- not as exciting. Walking should be pretty automatic for grown ups.

8:23am
FRENCH: I'm drunk.

8:23am
PADRAIC: Btw, now that your kid can walk- the next year is hell. Mazel Tov!

8:49am
JAKE: Bravo, Helene! Now get Daddy a beer!

ONE WEEK UNTIL BABY CLARA

6:34am

PADRAIC: Gentlemen- we are now a week from our due date. Prepare for the live play by play of the arrival of Clara. No detail will be left out. You will laugh, you will cry, you will shart your breeches. This is gonna get real.

6:55am

HENRY: Paderick best wishes my brother! Also Siri fuck you for not knowing how to spell Paderick. I mean I've been typing it for years and you still can't figure it out!

9:20am

MICHAEL: Padraic, have you considered live streaming the birth as well?
Also: LOVE the name!

9:24am

PADRAIC: cool! And there will be a live stream, alright. A literal stream of stuff in which there will be life.

10:53am

VICTOR: If we had a girl, we were going to name her Clara, after my grandmother. Thanks for screwing that up for us, Duffy!

11:28am

MICHAEL: No, Victor *heh* you can totally *snicker* use that name also. *giggle* I'm sure it's *heehee* fine.

11:39am

PADRAIC: Our third baby is gonna be named Victor Isaac.

11:40am

JAKE: Third? Junkies...

11:41am

FRENCH: Or you could go with Qlarrah?

11:48am

HENRY: Each of our babies from here on out will be named by daddy drinks majority vote.

1:28pm

HENRY: Qlarrah is solid. I vote qlarrah if a boy, victor Isaac if a girl.

2:19pm

PADRAIC: I think we are going to have a silent "victor" in her name. Like: "Clar(victor)a." I think that's pretty.

PRESCHOOL

PADRAIC: Guys- Freddy had his first day of preschool today. Made me just a wee bit cry-y in the eye area.
4:26pm

JAKE: Wow, you must be so excited to have so much free ti... oh, wait... sorry…
4:28pm

MICHAEL: #BabyBurn
4:30pm

PADRAIC: Exactly. And he is only doing 2 days a week, 3 hours a day. And every fourth day Freddy's there, one of us has to work there. Yippee!
4:30pm

MICHAEL: You Duffys are just full of great ideas.
4:30pm

PADRAIC: Baby burn is what your wife feels the first time you try to have sex after the birth.
4:31pm

4:32pm

VICTOR: Point. Duffy.

4:32pm

MICHAEL: The first time?

4:32pm

VICTOR: Point. Lanahan.

4:33pm

HENRY: Yeah nobody warned me about the burn.

4:35pm

MICHAEL: I think if you scroll through the back-log of this thread, you'll see that we did. In the most crass way possible.

5:26pm

HENRY: 😛

5:26pm

HENRY: Nope. Not the burn specifically. Lots of fore-shadowing but nothing about a burn.

Also that emoticon was a typeo. I do not approve of whatever that is.

12:39am

MICHAEL: I'm so excited to put Finley into Daycare and eventually Pre-school. Today we hit three places with one more this afternoon. And I already feel like I'm abandoning my little girl, and never want her to leave home. She's already going off to college in my mind.

12:41am

MICHAEL: One of the places was like Thunderdome. It took everything to be polite and ask our questions, before we ran screaming.

1:15am

VICTOR: By the way, if you have a silent "Victor" in your daughter's name, I'm going to pronounce it every time I say it.

And I may be the only one to sympathize about looking for daycare. It's the worst!

It's even worse up here, because we didn't start looking until a few months before he was born and then found out a lot of them have a year or two waiting list. Who the fuck waits 2 years to get into a day care! If I wait that long for my kid to get into your school, he better be fucking president when he gets out!

1:21am

MICHAEL: No shit!

Luckily the wait isn't that bad down here. We found a daycare that's great, right next door. Probably start there Sep.1, but because of when she was born, she won't be able to start Pre-school until NEXT September. Of course, I feel like who knows where we'll be or be living at that point...

Several Weeks Later...

9:39am

MICHAEL: Just dropped Finley off for a one-hour Daycare test run. And it was gut-wrenching. Oh, the look she gave me. This is gonna be tougher than I thought.

10:19am

VICTOR: Hang in there. It gets easier.

we stayed with him for like 1/2 hour the first time we dropped him off and I almost cried when we said goodbye He cried everyday for the first week or so until he got used to the place. Now, most times, he jumps out of my arms to go play with his buddies.

12:21pm

MICHAEL: Now, let me be clear: I was a mess dropping off and picking up. Finley couldn't have cared less either way. This fucking kid. ♥

12:35pm

PADRAIC: Freddy never cared. And while I felt a little emotional since it was a sign my little guy was getting older, I was also really excited to have three hours to read the paper and nap!

September 1st. First Day of Day Care...

9:12am

MICHAEL: Dropped Finley off for first full day of daycare. Devastating.

9:41am

VICTOR: "When you drop her off, you might feel a slight sting. That's guilt fucking with you. Fuck guilt! Guilt only hurts, it never helps. You fight through that shit. Cause two weeks from now, when you're napping on the couch in the middle of the day, you're going to say to yourself, 'Marcellus Wallis was right.'"

9:54am

MICHAEL: I needed that.
Fuck this guilt.
👍

9:55am

VICTOR: 👍

INDUCING WITH SEX

6:05pm
PADRAIC: Another day with no baby. 25 1/2 hours til the due date!

6:18pm
PADRAIC: Emily is convinced she has an African stone baby in her tummy, and is now wondering if pregnant is a permanent condition.

11:42am
MICHAEL: Padraic - you know the best way to kick-start labor: Doin' it. Worked for us!

12:11pm
PADRAIC: If I have sex with you, my baby is born? What's your address?!

12:21pm
MICHAEL: It's not gay if we're trying to labor a baby.

12:22pm
VICTOR: Or if you only suck the tip

12:22pm

MICHAEL: French also said he'd be happy to come over and yell profanities at Emily's belly to goad the baby out.

12:23pm

PADRAIC: Um, Victor. That's gay. Sucking the tip is still really gay.

12:23pm

VICTOR: No, it's not!

VICTOR'S STORY

VICTOR: I apologize in advance for the length of the next couple of messages.

I needed to get something out and it was going to take a while, so I wrote it out and will just paste it here.

Thanks for your understanding.

VICTOR: So, while we wait for Ms. Victor Duffy to be born, I have something I need to say.

Or I should say, come clean about. I've been trying to figure out a way and then the timing of how to tell you guys this for a while now. I felt bad because you all had shared a lot of painful things, and I was holding on to one.

Anyway, in short, Alex is a test tube baby. A real, bon-afide, grown in a petri dish kid.

Cindy and I had been trying to get pregnant for about a year and nothing was happening. It was about 6 months in that we started to suspect something was wrong.

So, at about 10 months in, I had a semen analysis done and we went to a fertility specialist. He said the semen was border line, but not too bad. So, he wanted to check Cindy out.

There are a number of tests and she was passing all of them with flying colors. The last thing to do was check the follicle count.

That was bad news. The doctor said Cindy had the

ovaries of a 47 year old woman. It looked like she only had 3 or 4 follicles working and we'd be lucky to get one good egg to work with.

To say Cindy was devastated is putting it mildly. So, like any good husband, I bought her the $300 mixer she wanted and we set out to get a second opinion.

We went to one of those fancy schmancy places in Beverly Hills and told the doctor our experience. He looked at the chart and said that everything looked good except the follicle count.

3:20pm

VICTOR: He asked when Cindy would start her cycle again. When we told him it was supposed to start at anytime, he looked at the chart again and asked when the follicle count had been done. We told him it was earlier that same week. He then tried to tactfully point out that you have to do the follicle count at the beginning of the cycle or you don't get an accurate count, because only some of the eggs grow and they squish the other follicles so you can't see them. I was fucking furious! The mental anguish that we had experienced in the last couple of days was completely unnecessary. Cindy spent the evenings crying, feeling like she had let me down, because she made us wait to have kids. It was terrible! And to top it off, I just bought a $300 mixer!

We were pissed, but elated. There was still hope. I'd never been more excited for Cindy to have her period.

So, it came and they did another follicle count and everything was fine! She had plenty of follicles. So it was just a matter of getting our baby making stuff together. We knew when she would be ovulating, so we made plans to do an IUI. (They take my stuff, "wash" it, then put it in her uterus, so it's got a good chance of making it.) And let me tell you, there is nothing better than going into an office and having a nurse lead you to a room and telling you to jerk off into a cup. Sarcasm.

3:21pm

VICTOR: Once they did the wash, we discovered my numbers weren't borderline. They were bad. There was a chance the IUI would work, but the doctor said it was a one in a million chance.

It didn't work. We grappled with what to do, but decided to give IUI another try. It didn't work again. The doctor suggested I go see a urologist to see if there was something functional that could be fixed. Let me tell you, there is nothing more enjoyable than having a doctor play with your balls for 15 minutes as he's trying to figure out what's wrong. Sarcasm.

Even better? I had to have an ultrasound. And having KY spread on your balls, while an older Korean woman examines them is a slice of heaven. Still sarcasm.

It turns out I have varicoceles. Varicose veins in the scrotum. Essentially, my balls were overheating and apparently had been for quite some time, because they are undersized and aren't producing sperm like they should. So, I've been using birth control all this time for nothing.

Great. There's an operation to fix it, but studies show it doesn't have much of an affect, if any, on fertility rates. So, there we were. We could keep trying and hopefully get lucky or spend a pretty decent amount of money on a science baby. Without going into detail, Cindy on hormones, was... uh... interesting. Yeah, let's go with that. Interesting. Once we did the first transfer, we had to wait to see if it took. It was heartbreaking when we found out she wasn't pregnant. So, we saddled up to try again. This time we put in two fertilized eggs and waited. They both took! We were having twins! ...for about 5 weeks. The second one just stopped growing, but we still had a good one going, so we weren't bothered.

3:22pm

VICTOR: The money we spent was absolutely worth it. The pain and disappointment of failed pregnancy attempts were nothing compared to the moment when Alex made his appearance in the world. I couldn't have been happier. Fortunately, unlike what Dr. Asshole said, we had 5 viable fertilized eggs to start with and we only used 3. So, the chance of Alex getting a sibling was pretty good. We just needed to decide when we wanted to have it.

CUT TO: In April Cindy sent me a text message asking if I had time to talk. It was a little odd, but what the hell, I called her. There was something in her voice that told me something was wrong, so I asked her "What's up?" She started stammering and saying how difficult it was

to tell me what she had to tell me. I was trying to keep it together, but honestly, I was freaking out. It felt like she was going to tell me that she fell in love with someone else and wanted a divorce. I wanted to tell her to spit it out, but didn't want to hear what she had to say, because I wasn't ready for my life to change.

Then she said the strangest thing. "I know you don't like me taking pregnancy tests when you're not around..." Why the hell was she talking about pregnancy test? " I was just driving myself crazy, because I hadn't had my period and I just wanted to know that I wasn't pregnant."

WHAT?!?!

"Victor, I'm pregnant."

Silence...

"Victor?"

Honestly, I was thinking, "Did she cheat on me and get pregnant by this other guy? No, she would never cheat on me! ...but how is she pregnant?"

3:22pm

VICTOR: "Victor?!?"

"Yeah. Sorry, I just....are you sure?"

"Yeah, I took two tests, but I'm going to buy a digital test on the way home to make sure. Yes, I'm pregnant. I'm having your baby, again."

"But, how?"

"I guess we just hit the lottery. Your guys got in there

and got me pregnant."

"Holy shit."

She did indeed buy a digital pregnancy test on the way home, but we wanted to wait until Alex was asleep before trying it. She had taken pictures of the other test results and sure as shit those lines were filled in. We didn't need the digital test. She was pregnant.

It was a wonderful surprise! Terrifying, but wonderful. For about 5 days. We found out she was pregnant on Thursday, but on Monday she started bleeding and it wouldn't stop. By the time she got to the doctor on Tuesday, she was positive she had a miscarriage. The doctor confirmed it. Even though we only knew for 5 days, it was still heartbreaking. Fate had taken the decision of deciding when we were going to try and have a second child out of our hands and it was quite freeing. Prior to finding out Cindy was pregnant, I had already started thinking about when we should try to have another. Also, I was trying to imagine what would happen if we were unsuccessful using the two fertilized eggs we still had.

So, her accidentally getting pregnant took the burden off and it felt wonderful. Oh well, we already had a beautiful son and we still had two eggs. Everything was still all right. We had our one in a million chance and it didn't work out.

3:22pm

VICTOR: CUT TO: Late May - I'm talking to a close friend of mine and he's the first person I tell about the pregnancy and the miscarriage. He tells me that after a miscarriage, women are really fertile. That's what the doctor told him after his wife had a miscarriage and lo and behold, she was pregnant the next month.

CUT TO: 5 days later - I walk in the door after work to see Cindy sitting in the recliner playing with Alex. She looks up at me and says, "I'm pregnant"

She remains pregnant today, my friends. 16 weeks to be exact. It's a boy and I'm thinking about naming him Qlarrah.

We aren't public yet, so, you know, #babylaw

3:23pm

VICTOR: Again, my apologies for the length.

3:44pm

PADRAIC: That was the biggest roller coaster of a story I have ever read! congrats!!!!!

4:04pm

HENRY: YES YES YES YES YES!!!! Congratulations victor!!! Mums the word. So filled with joy for you brother.

PADRAIC: I always believed in your balls, Victor. Always!

4:04pm

HENRY: I'm imagining them super tiny based on your story. Like marbles. The little kind.
Please don't start a balls photo challenge.

4:05pm

PADRAIC: Balls photos challenge!

4:06pm

HENRY: Fuck

4:06pm

VICTOR: #ballsphotochallenge
And thanks, gentlemen. It is an honor to serve with you

4:06pm

PADRAIC:

4:08pm

PADRAIC: Here are my balls and penis.
I know they look like a wasabi almond and two glass beads. But they are in fact, my genitals.

4:08pm

4:09pm

HENRY: Vic holy shit what you been through. So filled with joy for you.

4:11pm

HENRY: I haven't gotten to use these in a long time, do you think they're swollen?

4:13pm

PADRAIC: Victor- So touched you shared this with us, and so excited that it's such a happy happy ending! Hank- not quite as happy that you shared your sweet potato balls with us.

4:16pm

FRENCH: Victor! Congrats!!! Henry? For shame.

4:22pm

VICTOR: Gah!!! Henry's balls!!

People think I have a big dong because my balls are so small.

4:24pm

VICTOR:

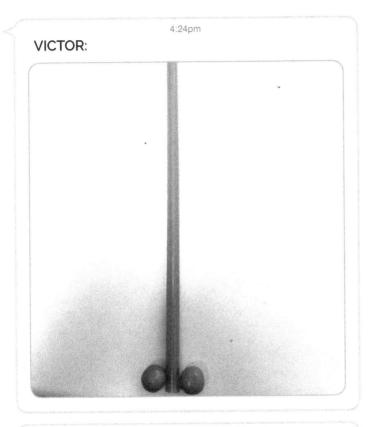

4:25pm

HENRY: Yeah. Soooo... Yep.
Laughing out loud Vic

4:26pm

PADRAIC: You could unlock a car door through a closed window with that thing.

4:26pm

HENRY: Sarah is gonna want to eat those sweet potatoes. And I'm being sadly literal.

4:27pm

VICTOR: Lol!!!

4:39pm

PADRAIC: I already ate my almond.

4:51pm

HENRY: At least someone did.

5:46pm

MICHAEL: Oh man, Victor, I'm SO sorry you guys had to go through all that. But happy ending indeed! (<--don't henry!)

5:46pm

HENRY: I just peeled m'sweet taters

9:51pm

MICHAEL: To scale, color, and shape:

9:51pm

MICHAEL:

10:28pm

VICTOR: Bwahaha!

OVERDUE

12:27am

PADRAIC: Well, the due date came and went. We'll see what happens tomorrow!

6:54pm

MICHAEL: French: Start yelling at that belly!

7:16pm

JAKE: Victor I finally got time to read your story... Craziness...Congratulations to you both!

7:26pm

FRENCH: There is something wrong with Victor and Paddy. I'm looking forward to my golden years with Vanessa and an entitled, socially inept, only child. I'm also going to home school her so I don't have to drive anywhere.

7:28pm

JAKE: 🙁 OK!

7:31pm

FRENCH: Don't Egg Man my feelings.

7:43pm
VICTOR: 😎????

7:45pm
PADRAIC: Looking "forward" to your golden years?

7:49pm
VICTOR: 👍

7:50pm
FRENCH: You fuckers! How dare you!

9:17pm
MICHAEL: I also look forward to your Golden Years, and bringing my only child over to your home. Our entitled, arrogant children will posture, not share, and I will drink all your booze. Cheers!

9:44pm
FRENCH: Finally. Reason.

12:00am
PADRAIC: I have a spelunkers helmet and tongs - I'm gonna get that kid out myself!

1:08am
JAKE: Are you sure you remember the way?

7:12am
VICTOR: I keep waking up expecting there to be a slew of messages. #babywatch

12:47pm
PADRAIC: We're on the second day overdue. Nothing yet, but we just had a check up yesterday, and everything seems cool. You guys will know when the first contraction hits!

2:18pm
HENRY: Where is your office Padraic? I need to know where do you work? I'd like to bring you guys these hand-medowns before the baby gets here if possible with my shoot schedule.

2:35pm
PADRAIC: I just work at home.

2:56pm
HENRY: What are you wearing right now?

PADRAIC: Vivienne Westwood.

4:36pm

HENRY: Hot.

5:44pm

MICHAEL: Anything?! Word on the street was you were at the hospital.

10:20pm

PADRAIC: Nothing yet.

Still at home.

10:21pm

VICTOR: Not even a false contraction?

10:22pm

MICHAEL: A watched pot doesn't boil. This baby needs some more time in the oven, and I can't blame her.

10:23pm

PADRAIC: Not a serious one. She's been having some periods of tightening over the past couple weeks, but not a real contraction

We're only 2 days over right now. Not too worried yet (but really ready)

10:23pm

FRENCH: I love you.

10:27pm

HENRY: Godspeed Paddy!!!

6:21am

CLARA'S BIRTH

8:58am
PADRAIC: Ok- we have had a bit of discharge. No contractions yet…

9:01am
MICHAEL: I don't ever want the word "discharge" to appear on Daddy Drinks again.

9:02am
PADRAIC: I'm warning you- this is gonna get real.

9:02am
FRENCH: Crap!

9:03am
PADRAIC: I'm a war correspondent, and I'm gonna take you onto THE BATTLEFIELD!

9:04am
VICTOR: Holy crap!

9:20am
HENRY: Let's do this!!!!
(I have nothing to do with it)
Go team!
(Again no credit due to me in this process)

9:31am
FRENCH: Paddys imbedded.

9:54am
PADRAIC: We're just gonna go about our day on high alert- we'll keep you posted

10:39am
VICTOR: Dittman you've been voted out.

10:44am
HENRY: What?!?!? I started this group!!!!
Nah you know what I accept the group's decision. And you two-baby-daddies out rank uni-baby-daddies, seems to me. Thanks for the memories, fellas.

2:15pm
VICTOR: Ok, we re-voted, you're back in.

5:19pm
PADRAIC: Contractions are starting. Here we go!

5:19pm
VICTOR: Eeeeeee!

5:19pm
HENRY: Yay yay yay! C'mon Duffys!!!!!

5:46pm
JAKE: You're welcome.

5:47pm
FRENCH: Poop that person!!!

6:29pm
MICHAEL: Go Team Duffy!!

6:39pm
PADRAIC: Mild contractions about 15 minutes apart…

6:45pm
HENRY: Gah!!!!!!!!!!!!!!!!!

PADRAIC: That gap was only 11 minutes. Holy crap. Now we're having dinner. She is a champ!

6:50pm

HENRY: It means so much to me to be included in updates! Daddy drinks!!!!! A toast to the duffys!!!

6:53pm

VICTOR: Holy cow! It's happening!!!!
Are you guys out to dinner?

6:55pm

HENRY: Here's to the duffys!

6:55pm

HENRY:

6:55pm

PADRAIC: We're just eating at home. The contractions are pretty mild, but the intervals are steadily going down. Who knows what that means- pass the pasta!

7:00pm

HENRY: Carbo-load padraic, you need your strength!!! *7:01pm*

VICTOR: To the Duffys! *7:05pm*

HENRY: 👍 *7:05pm*

HENRY: Wedding pic nice touch *7:06pm*

PADRAIC: You guys are the best! So Emily laid down and the contractions have backed off. So we're just waiting... *7:31pm*

HENRY: Victor spit your drink back in the bottle for gods sake! *7:32pm*

VICTOR: Ah crap *7:33pm*

PADRAIC: Whoops- turns out she's not pregnant. My bad! *7:33pm*

7:35pm

HENRY: Toasts back on!

7:39pm

PADRAIC: Water broke.

7:39pm

HENRY: Eeeeeeeeeeeeeeeee!

7:41pm

VICTOR: Her water broke?!?!? What are you in a movie?!?!

7:42pm

PADRAIC: I know!

7:43pm

HENRY: Water breaking is so classic!!!

7:52pm

PADRAIC: There's a stork- I see a stork on the roof!

7:56pm

MICHAEL: To. The. Duffys.

MICHAEL: 7:57pm

PADRAIC: Heading to the birth center. 6 min interval! 8:11pm

VICTOR: I'm so excited!!!! 8:16pm

HENRY: 👍 8:36pm

HENRY: First daddy drinks birth!!!! 8:37pm

PADRAIC: Just got to the birth center! 8:43pm

HENRY: Godspeed brother. Dittmans passing out but I'll be up every 3-4 hours to check on ya!! Jake get your toast on!!!! 8:43pm

JAKE: 👍 8:45pm

PADRAIC: There's a bathtub! Would it be wrong if I took a quick one? 8:56pm

9:02pm
VICTOR: If I remember correctly, you're supposed to be relaxed for the birth and taking a bath helps you relax. So, I say it's wrong if you don't take one.

9:02pm
HENRY: Emily should want you to feel good.

9:06pm
PADRAIC: I keep trying to relax, but this lady keeps moaning next to me.

9:19pm
VICTOR: Tell her to pipe down!

9:47pm
PADRAIC: Birth is hard. This can't be the most efficient way to make new people.

9:57pm
PADRAIC: Lots of back labor.

9:58pm
VICTOR: Oh no! Back labor is no fucking joke. That's how it started for Cindy with Alex. We thought something was wrong. Nope! Just really fucking painful back labor.

9:59pm
MICHAEL: Ugh...Angela had back labor for HOURS. I'm feelin' for her. ☺
She can get through it!

10:12pm
PADRAIC: She's a little dehydrated, so we're starting an IV. Nothing to worry about...

10:13pm
MICHAEL: Keep mopping that brow, and keeping her relaxed. Yoga breathing!

10:18pm
PADRAIC: I feel like crying- she is awesome.

10:29pm
HENRY: I'm on my way.

10:40pm

PADRAIC: IV drip brought the fetal heart rate down a bit, which is a good thing. Everything's looking good…

10:41pm

VICTOR: Sweet!

10:43pm

MICHAEL: Weep, you sonovabitch! You're human and God knows I did!

Goodnight, Sweet Duffy's. Keep the live posts coming - we'll keep checking in through the middle of the night.

11:23pm

PADRAIC: In the bath! Forgot the dinosaurs and Noah's ark.

11:53pm

VICTOR: Dammit, Duffy! You had one job!!!

12:26am

FRENCH: Only advice? Don't talk too much. She knows she should breath. And push. Squeeze her hand, don't make eye contact, and shut your yap.

12:36am

PADRAIC: She's out! She's gorgeous and Emily pushed her out like a champ!!!!!!

12:37am

VICTOR: Congratulations!!!!!
Holy shit that was fast!!!!

12:38am

FRENCH: Beautiful, Paddy. Just beautiful. Weight? Name?

12:55am

PADRAIC: Clara Elizabeth Duffy. Don't know weight yet!

1:17am

JAKE: I've been wondering for years why I was saving this...

1:18am

JAKE: I would've cracked another beer, but then I'd have to pee like a pregnant woman all night long...

1:47am

PADRAIC: She's latched. Btw, she has a ton of hair. Freddy was 2 years old before he had this much hair.

1:53am

JAKE: You have great fortune with the birthing of children, Duffy... You should probably just keep doing it... I'm calling 11 months from today for #3: Who's in?

Just a pick-the-date pool, by the way... I'm not giving odds...

1:58am

PADRAIC: 5 hours of labor including 28 minutes of pushing.

4:07am

PADRAIC: 7.5. And we are now home, snug in our beds. And it feels like a crazy dream...

5:20am

HENRY: I think we can all agree. It's all a crazy dream. #babylaw

Side note that shot of you all throwing your babies is AMAZING. sorry we missed the party and the photo op! I'm guessing that's the moment I was voted out.

MICHAEL: Yes! Congrats, Paddy!! Well done, sir - our love to the lady!

7:08am

MICHAEL: In the spirit of welcoming a new life into our group, I'd like to vote to welcome Henry back into DD.

7:31am

JAKE: Victor let him back in about an hour after the party... No discipline, that one...

9:09am

VICTOR: What can I say? I'm a softie...

9:13am

MICHAEL: A handsome softie.

9:13am

HENRY: I'm back out. It's all good. #babylaw Padraic she's beautiful.

9:53am

VICTOR: Did I miss a picture?!!?

10:05am

10:13am

JAKE: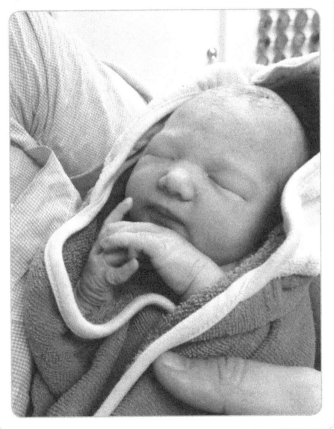

10:19am
VICTOR: YAY!!!!
She's beautiful!!!

11:08am
MICHAEL: What a perfect beauty! Congrats, brother.

2:05pm
PADRAIC: And Freddy is being such a sweet big brother. Thanks so much for all the support, gentlemen. There's only one more thing to do...

...A toast picture from French.

2:08pm
MICHAEL: 👍

2:11pm
VICTOR: 👍

2:41pm
HENRY: 👍

2:41pm
HENRY: Wait I'm still out right?

2:47pm
VICTOR: No, we let you back in.

2:47pm
JAKE: Or more accurately, we keep pulling you back in...

ONE DAY LATER...

7:35pm
HENRY: where is French's toast?

11:16am
FRENCH: Toast?

11:24am
VICTOR: During the birth of ClarVictora Duffy (The Victor is silent) we all took pictures with a glass toasting to the Duffy's. Half of us had something that said "Dad" on it....

11:28am
PADRAIC: Where am I? Who are you guys?! Aaaah!

11:28am
VICTOR: Padraic!!!
24 hours in, how is it the second time?!?!

12:50pm
MICHAEL: Padraic! Go towards the light!!

10:46pm

PADRAIC: We'll, you're not as stressed, because you kinda know what you're doing. But boy am I tired. Even with Grandma here (only until Saturday!) taking care of a three year old and a newborn is really, really hard. And the world doesn't give you nearly as long to nest. With Freddy, we hid from the world for two weeks. I had yesterday. And now I am frantically trying to work and answer emails in what little time I have.

10:48pm

PADRAIC: But listening to your toddler softly sing a lullaby to your little baby girl makes it worth it. But when grandma leaves, I'm gonna order me a Ukrainian Internet bride. "Freddy- that's your second mommy, the mommy who will do the laundry and pick you up from pre-school."

11:14pm

JAKE: ... and tuck Daddy in for naptime...

12:06am

VICTOR: Well now I'm terrified...

10:12pm

PADRAIC: Grandma leaves on Saturday, and I don't even understand how Sunday will work. I don't think I'm ever gonna see anyone ever again. But it IS making me even more determined to make things happen. If I have to sleep three hours a night, I'm gonna write plays, and create!

10:23pm

FRENCH: Do you need food on Sunday? We can just place it on your porch.

10:32pm

MICHAEL: What. Can. We. Do?! Food? Supplies? Porn? Ask and ye shall receive.

9:53am

FRENCH: And here's your toast. You are what you eat. A burnt out heel. Blammo!

TWO WEEKS LATER...

MICHAEL: Checking in, Paddy. How are you all doing a couple a weeks in, sans gramma??
10:24pm

HENRY: Been swamped with auditions and work haven't forgotten ya duffies!
7:01am

VICTOR: ...Padraic? Are you there?
10:32am

MICHAEL: My favorite memory of Padraic from when he was alive: when he thought he could have a second child, manage a theatre company, and continue to write plays and NOT die.

Pretty funny in retrospect.
11:03am

JAKE: 👍
11:12am

VICTOR: Yeah, that was pretty silly of him to think all of that wouldn't kill him. I'll miss his awkward dancing most of all...
11:12am

5:56pm

PADRAIC: I just bought this phone at a swap meet. Seems the previous owner was eaten by his own children. Who are y'all?

5:57pm

HENRY: Well this will be an improvement over the last guy, welcome stranger!

5:57pm

FRENCH: Goddammit.

VAGINA POOP

9:06am
PADRAIC: Poop. #babyvagina

9:08am
MICHAEL: I've logged so many hours getting poop out of that baby vagina, I should have my license. My Vagina-Poop- Scooping license.

9:08am
JAKE: Yeah. That.

9:09am
PADRAIC: How did humans not go extinct? They poop in their own vagina? Unacceptable.

9:11am
JAKE: Especially when it's a loose stool, and you don't catch it right away, and she's been squishing it around for awhile... that's when you gotta go waaaay up in there to clean it out...

9:11am
HENRY: The hell is going on here???

9:12am

HENRY: Wait. Gravity pulls that poop out EVENTU- ALLY, right?

9:12am

JAKE: freakin' #babyvagina spelunking...
No, Henry, you do...

9:13am

PADRAIC: Btw, I plopped Freddy down in front of the TV so I could message you guys about parenting. Ah, the irony...

9:13am

JAKE: 👍

9:13am

HENRY: Shit.

9:15am

JAKE: It takes a very steady hand...

9:16am

PADRAIC: ...To clean poop from a #babyvagina

11:26am

PADRAIC: And while I'm ranting- was the baby vagina DESIGNED to hold poop? That's all I do now- wipe baby mustard out of little lady parts.

11:28am

FRENCH: Go front to back.

11:28am

MICHAEL: You WILL be scooping poop out of that vagina for the next three years of your life.

11:29am

PADRAIC: They should make vagina covers.

11:29am

MICHAEL: front to back, back to front - doesn't make a difference. The poop is already in that vagina.

11:29am

FRENCH: Let's start a vagina cover band. Songs?

11:33am

PADRAIC: Ring of fire.

11:34am

MICHAEL: In this instance the "Ring of Fire" is the vagina.

That's in case Henry wasn't following the conversation. Henry?

11:35am

FRENCH: Did the Beatles write a song called "poop puss?"

11:39am

MICHAEL: Feels right.

11:40am

VICTOR: "Feels right" is the song or "poop puss" feels right?

11:41am

PADRAIC: yellow submarine, where "yellow" means yellow and "Submarine" means poop in a baby vagina.

11:41am

FRENCH: Horrid.

Just awful.

11:45am

MICHAEL: Well, Octopus's Garden seems apropos.

11:46am

FRENCH: You're a terrible pig.

11:46am

MICHAEL: Praise from Caesar.

11:47am

PADRAIC: Lovely Rita, your vagina is full of shit.

11:51am

FRENCH: It's Sunday morning. Fuck all of you. Every last one.

11:52am

PADRAIC: Grumpy French makes me giggle.

12:17pm

VICTOR: Where the hell is Dittman?

12:48pm

FRENCH: A solid question.
Probably sanitizing some small, murky, lady bits.

SLEEP TRAINING

HENRY: My dudes. We are starting to sleep train. To be clear, I mean using the no cry method so it's a longer process with slow steps as opposed to the cry it out methods. We're starting now because if we aren't seeing progress by 8 months we might try a cry it out. What did you guys do and when? Looking for your experiences pals.

FRENCH: For us, bedtime was key. Bath at 8:00. Then one of us would sit with her and gas her out with milk and soft 70's tunes. It let her know it was time for the "long, dark nap.'

She'd usually wake up at about two. I'd make a half milk/water, soft music and put her back. If she cried, I'd let her work it out for awhile. If it was going to crap, I'd try again. We did this a few weeks with a plan that after that she'd just cry it out but she naturally just started sleeping through. Some nights better than others, but…

MICHAEL: Our deal was similar with a standard bedtime ritual - moving to solid foods helped her extend a bit at night as well. But after nine months she was still getting up once between 4-5am for a bottle of milk. So we did the 5 nights of going in a humming while rubbing her back until she went to sleep. Often times it took 30-45 minutes of that, and then you were back in the room

20 minutes later. But eventually that worked and she learned to sooth herself back to sleep after that wake-up.

9:33am

PADRAIC: We moved Freddy from a pack-and- play in our room to a crib in his own room at 3 months. It was actually Emily's decision- I would have kept him in our room longer. But I think it made things easier. He was so young, that he hadn't gotten a ton of bad habits. So for a little while he did great. Then at about 4 months he had a bit of regression and started to cry a bunch. So for a couple months we became sleep ninjas. It would take a good 45 minutes from when he was in his crib lights out to when he would fall asleep - I would crouch on the floor, my finger in his mouth, while my arm slowly went dead. The noise machine roaring like an angry ocean right by his head. Then, when he would FINALLY fall asleep, I would slowly crawl out of the room on my hands and knees, every creak of the carpeted floor echoing through the house. Not exaggerating, sometimes it would take me five minutes to go ten feet.

And then he would wake up, and I would start all over. At around 5 or 6 months, we had had enough - we started sleep training. We would let him cry for 5 minutes, then go in a soothe him. Then ten minutes (it wasn't quite that clinical- we just sussed it out.) And then there was a tiny period of time when Emily and I would sit exhausted in the hallway at 3 in the morning right outside his door while he screamed himself to sleep. But that didn't last very long.

Since then, it has been a series of slowly-developing bad habits to our rules and then a short but painful correction. So Freddy would every so often sneak into our room in the middle of the night to cosleep, and because we were exhausted (and it's really sweet to snuggle) we would let him. Then after a while, we realized he was doing it every night. That was a hard bad habit to correct!

10:03am

JAKE: We've mostly let her establish the pattern, and then enforced it when she varies into crankypants. Now if she gets enough exercise and a full dinner, she sleeps through. If not, she wakes up, but only for a milk top-up.

10:58am

VICTOR: And for the record, unless you have a family bed, transitioning your child to another sleep situation is going to involve some crying. You're going to feel horrible, but it doesn't last very long and they still love you and don't remember.

10:59am

PADRAIC: When it comes to crying, I have found it helpful for me to separate it into two kinds: scared and angry. I can ignore angry crying all night, but if he is scared, I'm in his room in a heartbeat. And if he sheds the tears of a stripper, I shower him with dollar bills, yo!

11:26am

MICHAEL: We found that Finley would sleep the same whether she was in her vibrating chair, our arms, and the co-sleeper. And since we were adamant about our bedroom being our space, we started putting her in the crib in her room as of 3 months. She really had no problems at all. We were lucky in that regard I think. That also allowed one of us to be "On Duty" and the other could stay asleep in our bedroom.

11:58am

JAKE: We had a bassinet next to the futon, where Crystal slept for the first couple months, and I would too unless I needed a night of sleep. Then we started taking turns…

12:18pm

HENRY: Honestly we've been willy nilly on nighttime patterns (though very consistent on prebed ritual) so I expected this to be a mess to start. We'll get there. I'm loving hearing your stories especially because it makes me feel less like we screwed up or like I'm alone in this bizarre half-sleep nightlight-lit world I'm inhabiting last week or so.

12:33pm

VICTOR: Yeah, "pattern" takes on a whole new meaning during this time. You'll find yourself calling something a pattern after a day and a half and then later realize how ridiculous it was to think it was a pattern.

12:50pm

VICTOR: Alex would have breaks in sleeping patterns right before developing a new "skill"

He still does. Like he would be sleeping ok, then a few nights or week of not good sleep and then he rolled over for the first time. Same thing before crawling, walking, picking up things and recently saying words. I'll have to find out where that info came from, so it doesn't seem like I'm pulling it out of my ass.

MICHAEL: Honestly, it'll just go like that for another week, maybe two, and then it'll change into something else. The one thing I'll never forget, is that the moment I began to get used to something, or even count on it, it would change. It's a total mindfuck. It's where you start to lose your sanity.

12:53pm

MICHAEL: Stay patient, brother. And stay fluid. You have to be.

2:04pm

VICTOR: We started with Alex in our room in the bassinet. When he got too big for that it was a bit too emotional for Cindy to put him in a different room, so we started co-sleeping, which in a way was nice because she could feed him on demand without getting up. By then he was no longer taking a bottle, so I was no longer feeding him. Then when that got old, we put the crib mattress on the bed next to us so he could get used to sleeping on it. And what happened is Cindy just slept on the ground with him. Then we moved the mattress into his room on the floor, and he immediately started rolling over, so we couldn't leave him alone on it. So, we started co-sleeping again until Cindy could find a sleep consultant who she trusted to tell us that letting Alex cry for 10 minutes wasn't ruining his brain. The plan was to go in every 10

minutes for 30 seconds until he went down. I was all for it, but knew it would be tough.

We started on a Friday and I took Monday off in preparation for tiredness. Friday night as I prepared to put him down, Cindy went for a walk, because she couldn't handle it. I went in twice and at 29 minutes, he fell asleep. He only woke up twice that night and was back to sleep within a half an hour. The next night he fell asleep after 15 minutes and only woke up once. The next night he slept through the night. So it was WAY easier than I thought it was going to be and took just 2 days really.

2:11pm

JAKE: At like 3 months she started doing 8 hours solid at night, midnight to 8am... We assumed we were geniuses and all other parents were stupid... That lasted until about 18 months, when she started needing feedings... now she's down between 8 and 9, usually up once around midnight or 1 needing a little soothing/bottle, and then down again until 7-ish... We never really followed a plan from a book or anything, just kind of feeling it out, for better or worse... We stay as consistent as possible with the nighttime ritual, but we also aren't religious about it... I mean we're strict with it when we're home in the evening, but sometimes we're not, and we don't worry about it too much...

2:23pm

HENRY: THANK YOU for the help daddies, it was wonderful to grasp at my phone last night and know cavalry was on the way. #BabyLaw.

Now, who wants to watch my baby tonight from 8pm until 3pm Monday?

POOPS FOR SCOOPS

10:54pm

PADRAIC: I made a deal with my son: if he shits 5 times in the toilet, I'll buy him an ice cream cone. I call it "Poops for Scoops."

I wish I was making this up.

11:03pm

VICTOR: Is it five times in a row, or just five times?

11:05pm

PADRAIC: Just five times. Don't have to be in a row. We have a chart. Poop in the potty? Get a sticker. 5 stickers? Ice cream.

11:08pm

FRENCH: I want that deal.

11:12pm

VICTOR: When does the deal stop? Or will you one day say to his first serious girlfriend, "Look, you're going to have to take over the scoops for poops deal."

11:19pm

PADRAIC: If any of you poop in my toilet 5 times, I'll buy you ice cream.

11:20pm
JAKE: On my way…

11:21pm
VICTOR: Is this deal retroactive? Asking for a friend.

11:21pm
FRENCH: Crap. I just pooped. And now I feel I'm behind the 8 ball with the other guys.

11:21pm
MICHAEL: What about secret poops I've already laid around your property?

11:23pm
FRENCH: Can I poop and bring it to your wife?

11:24pm
PADRAIC: It's gotta be in the toilet. That's the whole point. Freddy's been shitting everywhere but the toilet. And I can't take it anymore. Cause now I have another kid that shits like a cat with food poisoning.

11:24pm
FRENCH: Got it.

11:25pm
MICHAEL: Sounds like you've raised a real prince. A poop-prince.

11:25pm
FRENCH: Can I shit in your face?

11:26pm
PADRAIC: If it's on the toilet.

11:26pm
MICHAEL: French! Padraic!

11:26pm
FRENCH: Mike!

11:26pm
MICHAEL: French!

11:27pm

FRENCH: Victor!

11:27pm

JAKE: I'm no longer on my way…

11:27pm

FRENCH: Jake!

11:27pm

MICHAEL: Jake!

FUCK YOU, DAYLIGHT SAVING TIME

9:25am

MICHAEL: Thankfully, this time wasn't as bad as the last, but I'd just like to say: Fuck You, Daylight Saving!

9:26am

HENRY: For us it was actually lucky that it fell on Halloween weekend because Halloween screwed up her sleep schedule so much anyway. Plus she learned to stand up this weekend- all of that combined, everything was out the fucking window.

11:40am

PADRAIC: Daylight saving was awesome! I take the middle of the night shift, so the hour I was feeding didn't exist! And then Emily takes the first shift, so I didn't have to wake up with the kids when they got up early because of the time change! I WIN!

12:23pm

HENRY: WINNER!!! Take that, love of your life and mother of your children!!

THE EMERGENCY ROOM

2:12am

PADRAIC: Well, we are currently in the middle of our first emergency room visit with Clara. (I'm home with Freddy.) Freddy brought home a head cold, which we all got, including Clara. But then everybody one by one got better, but Clara's lingered as a dry cough. Then it turned wet, (but she was still happy, eating and sleeping well, no fever). Well she woke up today miserable, (still no fever), but by the afternoon had mellowed out. Tonight: fever. Coughing. Inconsolable.

Green poop. So off to the middle of the night emergency room!

2:15am

PADRAIC: When I left for the theater, they were asleep, relaxed, and I was ready to get a text at any moment in case Clara suddenly got worse. (I can be home in less than ten minutes). The text came when I was halfway home.

2:15am

VICTOR: Fuck! That's my nightmare.

3:09am

HENRY: Fuck

MICHAEL: Is she okay now?! Keep us posted.

8:05am

HENRY: Update? You okay Paddy?

8:56am

PADRAIC: Yes- we're good. I'll give an update in just a little bit…

9:15am

PADRAIC: So the doctor at the ER thinks it's a virus, so they sent us home. And I think the whole ER experience exhausted Clara so much, that she slept like a baby when she got home.

10:36am

What's frustrating is that even with health insurance, ERs are always a big expense. And sadly, cost is definitely part of the calculus of whether you bring your kid in. And (thankfully) every single time we have gone into the ER or the doctor because of a sickness or injury, we should not have. In hindsight, I should have rocked her until she fell asleep. Because now, when we are really pinching our pennies , we have a $200 co-pay and who knows what for the chest x-ray, etc. Those middle of the night decisions are always hard - I wish we weren't always financially punished for being safe rather than sorry.

HENRY: Sucks man. So sorry brother. But so glad you're all safe. It's a tough call when waiting is the unknown and perhaps safe is better than sorry. Still, sucks.

1:14pm

FRENCH: Oy. The worst.

1:18pm

VICTOR: Totally. I feel so fortunate that Alex's worst sick times have come during the day when we could take him to the doctor. There have been times when I wouldn't have hesitated to take him to the ER if the doctor's office wasn't open.

1:30pm

PADRAIC: I find myself disappointed that it wasn't bacterial- if it were, we would have been "right" to bring her in, and they could have given something to her. Silly thing to think…

1:36pm

And it would have been a lot less expensive if we would have just gone in to the doctor on Friday when we first got concerned about her cough. But we try not to over react. But Clara's little face has been given me a whole lot of smiles today. And that's all that matters in the world.

Now I just hope hope hope we don't have the late afternoon fever flare up. I got both kids from 3-9pm. ☺

HENRY: Prayers dude.

1:45pm

MICHAEL: You WERE right to bring her in. Always better safe than sorry.

We'll start a kickstarter for you.

2:40pm

JAKE: That's such a scary time... I'm so glad everyone's OK... Crystal's been suggesting I drink less because we're so poor... Preposterous...

9:47pm

MICHAEL: *sigh* it's the first to go....

9:55pm

HENRY: It shouldn't be.

10:08pm

JAKE: The other day Lola (the dog) lost a tooth... Semele found it on the ground and tried to give it to her... "Here Lola!" I saw something gross in her hand and grabbed it... after contemplating this weird bone thing for a moment, I realized it was a tooth, and I pried Lola's jaws open to look... In the upper left was a big gaping flesh-hole where a molar should be... Crystal was super bummed, and wanted to take her to the vet... Our dog is about to turn 13, so I talked her out of it... It's only one tooth, and she's not in any distress in any other way, still eating, etc... I didn't want to pay $ to have the vet tell me our dog is old... and I didn't want to do that because I know sometimes we'll have to do it for our daughter... You can't second-guess after the fact, you make the call and handle the consequences...

That's why you're the dad...

11:38pm

PADRAIC: I did feel like the "Dad" at the time. Emily, who is always strong and in control, was exhausted and didn't know what to do. I felt like I had to make the call. And while I didn't like the situation, I liked taking control of it. It's like when I get emotional every time I tell Freddy that it's my job to keep him safe. There's something in our DNA that makes you feel fulfilled when you are protecting them.

6:07am

7:32am

HENRY: We've spent a lot of time talking about taking care of babies and being daddies. These emergency room and dog care questions are about being Dad, those tough questions the family looks to the Father to answer. You guys made the best call you could at the time and I'm sure Emily, Crystal and the kids are very happy to have you standing up to make those calls. Love you guys.

HALLOWEEN

HENRY: Just get on the stick and post your kids' Halloween costume pics already, guys.

HENRY:

4:03pm

HENRY:

5:19pm

FRENCH: A cat.

6:27pm

HENRY: YES!

6:30pm

PADRAIC: Wonder Woman nursing batgirl.

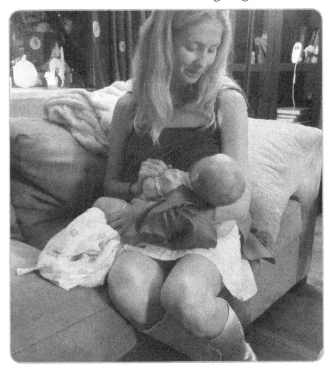

6:35pm

PADRAIC: And here is batman and batgirl.

6:36pm

PADRAIC:

> **PADRAIC:** Are you guys just loving your family right now? Because I am. Our families are awesome, gentlemen.
>
> *6:50pm*

> **FRENCH:** It's really fun.
>
> *6:56pm*

VICTOR: Picture #1

7:17pm

VICTOR: Picture #2

7:18pm

7:19pm

VICTOR: Yep. We're having a ball.

7:49pm

HENRY: Isaacs!!!! Amazing. Duffy are you Robin?????? Lanahan is Finley in her dragon suit???

7:50pm

HENRY: Our street in Burbank is so amazing for trick-or-treaters there's tons of kids everywhere and all you can hear up and down the street is kids laughing and yelling trick-or-treat and saying please and thank you it's just like a throwback to the 1950s. I love living in the suburbs. We took Hannah to two or three houses and now she is asleep and we are getting cozy, I'm really excited for when she is old enough to know what is going on.

8:40am

FRENCH:

8:51am

HENRY: Oh my god French. She was a cat and you were the mouse??? Adorable.

Lanahan? Jake?

1:01pm

MICHAEL: We took Dragon to the Redondo Family Halloween Fair! For the most part the Dragon wasn't having it.

1:02pm

MICHAEL:

1:14pm

HENRY: Amazing costume!!!

2:13pm

FRENCH: I love it.
Love it.

10:40am

JAKE:

10:41am

JAKE: Downtown Kids Fair = Bullshit Stress Fest!

10:41am

HENRY: HA!!! Well she's adorable so you got that to fall back on.

Outtakes— Stuff That Didn't Make the Book... and Maybe Still Shouldn't

---

FRENCH:
5:21pm
I'm currently experiencing a baby-free Labor Day Weekend. And that gives me a boner.

PADRAIC: I remember boners.
5:22pm

JAKE: Mine are in Scottsdale.
5:53pm
Family, not boners.

MICHAEL: Nobody wants their boner to end up in Scottsdale.
5:54pm

****

8:47pm

JAKE: How's everyone's holiday going? I just ate soup from a can!

9:04pm

FRENCH: A tin can? Or a woman's can?

Big, fun difference.

9:07pm

JAKE: un-fun…

9:08pm

FRENCH: Aw!

****

11:12pm

MICHAEL: Baby is with Gramma & Granpa for the weekend. My wife is still here. Servicing my boners*.

11:12pm

MICHAEL: *She still won't service my boners

11:15pm

PADRAIC: I want boner service!

11:15pm

FRENCH: Are we talking ice cream or boners?

11:16pm

MICHAEL: If pornography has taught me anything, it's that boners are like ice cream to ladies.

11:16pm

PADRAIC: My boners taste like ice cream.

Terrible, penis flavored ice cream.

11:17pm

MICHAEL: 

****

VICTOR: Tonight in the bathtub Alex found his penis, like you do. He started playing with it and giggling, like you do. Then he started trying to kiss it, like...you wish you could do. He bent over as far as he could as said "mwah! Penis besos." True story.

9:48pm

MICHAEL: Beer has just come through my nose.

10:18pm

****

HENRY: Here's something I did not know. When you actually get a night in a hotel without the baby, free to sleep from 10p-6a? You still wake up.

You still. Wake up. All night.

And sometimes the ceiling fan sounds like your daughter's crying.

6:56am

FRENCH: Sometimes if I listen to the baby monitor just right I can convince myself there's a ghost in the nursery. Also Vanessa's breast pump was an unapologetic racist.

7:01am

MICHAEL: Oh, yeah. I should have recommended sleeping pills for those first free nights of sleep. You need the nudge.

7:59am

VICTOR: ...wait...I need to hear how the breast pump was racist...?

8:12am

****

MICHAEL: After our nanny got Finley sick, I gave the nanny herpes. I'm pretty sure I won that round.

2:01pm

HENRY: The ol' Lanahan Infected Weiner Punch.

2:08pm

****

12:18am

PADRAIC: Freddy and I had a farting contest today. He shit his pants. I win.

7:00am

HENRY: Freddy won.

****

11:53pm

FRENCH: When I gas my baby to sleep with warm milk and Van Morrison? I feel like a champion of bedtime.

1:59am

JAKE: Do you offer that service for adults?

4:55am

FRENCH: $300. No eye contact.

7:15am

HENRY: Can I get the eye contact rate?

11:54am

FRENCH: $1,400

11:55a

HENRY: 👍

****

4:22pm

PADRAIC: I'm at Legoland right now lying on plastic grass listening to techno music surrounded by tiny buildings. I feel like a giant on acid.

4:28pm

FRENCH: Did you take a hit of E? Or are you with your kid?

4:55pm

PADRAIC: Wait- it was either/or? Whoops. um…

****

3:21am

HENRY: You know what sucks? Wife asleep. BABY asleep. Daddy... Full on insomnia. And every hour that goes by I'm closer to needing to be alert and awake to take care of said baby. DANG.

8:13am

PADRAIC: I've been there. Try a bottle of NyQuil and punching yourself in the face.

****

7:56pm

HENRY: I call this one "baby hates tutu."

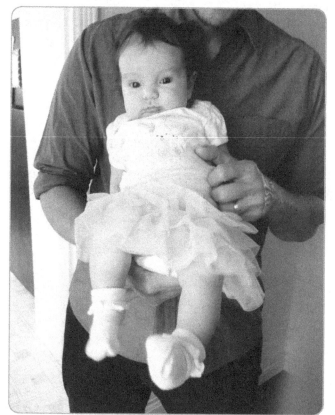

9:01pm

MICHAEL: I call this one "baby loves trash."

2:43am

FRENCH: Helene learned to clap today and is very pleased with herself. So much so that we're clapping at 2:45am. My baby and I have a wicked case of the clap.

2:51am

FRENCH: We also both have a venereal disease. They grow up so fast.

****

2:42pm

JAKE: Wait I got another one:

Please don't pee in my face while I'm cleaning up your poop.

2:47pm

FRENCH: Bad manners.

Also: Don't throw up in my mouth during the Airplane Game.

****

****

VICTOR: Me: They are for more than just milk, son.
Alex: Shut the fuck up?!?
Me: Seriously.

8:05pm

JAKE: 👍

9:07pm

HENRY: 👍

9:10pm

****

PADRAIC: fsdfgbmbnjhjjjhhnhhhnnfbnuuuoqwerrrfff-hgrfcsdghlijhjhjhnijkjnnjhhfsxdv

Guys- this conversation is no longer secure- a baby got in!

7:03pm

FRENCH: 👍 👍 👍

7:07pm

PADRAIC: And I'm not even kidding. I go over to see what he's doing on the iPad, and he's got Daddy Drinks open and he's typing away. So of course, I just hit send.

7:08pm

****

8:31pm

FRENCH: Helene just crawled over, stood up like a monkey and looked at me for 10 seconds. Then she plopped back on the floor. I'm officially terrified. Anyone?

8:42pm

HENRY: Dear Lord, French, just give her whatever she wants and avoid eye contact. If that fails make yourself bigger and louder than her and don't show fear!!!!!!

8:44pm

FRENCH: Or do I make myself small. Like with a bear.

8:52pm

HENRY: Dude I don't fuckin know but you gotta do something and do it soon.

8:59pm

FRENCH: She's in the cage or crib or...I don't know.

9:56pm

HENRY: Don't take your eyes off her for Pete's sake!

9:56pm

MICHAEL: She knows what she did.

10:10pm

MICHAEL: You break Baby Law, you go to Baby Jail

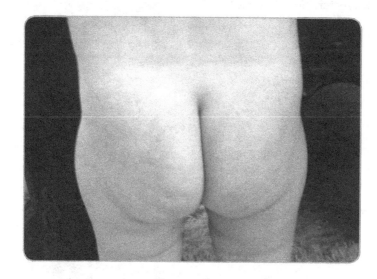

——— THE END ———

ABOUT THE AUTHORS

HENRY

HENRY DITTMAN used to have a career as a working actor on shows such as *Mad Men*, *Entourage*, and *CSI: Cyber*; acting in over 100 television commercials; and spending free time performing award-winning roles in award-winning theater productions with his pals. He went surfing daily, took his wife on spur-of-the-moment vacations, and had NBA season tickets for 14 years—just for fun! Then he became a father, and things completely went to hell.

PADRAIC

PADRAIC DUFFY is the Managing Director of The Sacred Fools Theater in Los Angeles and occasionally a playwright when he's not being vomited on by his wonderful children. Not an actor himself, he is happily surrounded by them: his talented wife, his Daddy Drinks buddies, his father and brother, and his son, who looked him right in the eye and said, "I did not poop my pants." (Spoiler: he did.)

VICTOR

VICTOR ISAAC was born a skinny black man. He stopped being skinny shortly after becoming a father. Coincidence? Probably. When not being father, Victor creates art at Sacred Fools Theater. He can be found most Saturday nights hosting "Serial Killers at Sacred Fools Theater" and drinking tequila.

MICHAEL

JAKE

MICHAEL LANAHAN is a husband, father, and actor. His dream to be a stay-at-home dad bit him in the butt, and he's been losing his mind ever since. He often refers to his daughter as the "little terrorist," "poop princess," and "hey, you." Mike has been seen on *The Office*, *Rizzoli & Isles*, and *Jersey Boys*, as well as plays in LA & Off Broadway. He dedicates this book to Finley: First she took him hostage, and now she's the love of his life. Maybe that's the Stockholm Syndrome.

JACOB SIDNEY was recently awarded FATHER OF THE YEAR for teaching his 4-year-old how to get him beers from the fridge during football games. He is author of the full-length solo show called "A Sweet Deal," as well as numerous short plays, songs, and vocal arrangements. In addition to a long stage acting career, Sidney works as Marketing Director for Ojai Playwrights Conference.

FRENCH

FRENCH STEWART became a father shortly after being told by doctors that he had "the most useless seed the medical community had ever witnessed." Take that, science! His role on *Third Rock from the Sun* made him a "national treasure" (his words). Since then he can be seen in *Inspector Gadget 2, Home Alone 4, Beverly Hills Chihuahua 2* or any sequel to a children's movie that none of the original cast members want anything to do with.